HUNTING THE
WHITETAIL DEER

HUNTING THE WHITETAIL DEER

How to Bring Home
North America's No. 1
Big-Game Animal

Norm Nelson

David McKay Company, Inc.
NEW YORK

Library of Congress Cataloging in Publication Data

Nelson, Norm.
  Hunting the whitetail deer.

  Includes index.
  1. White-tailed deer hunting. I. Title.
SK301.N34   799.2′77357   80-14449
ISBN 0-679-51084-2

Dedicated to
Dad and Uncle Ralph.
The old-timers are the best-timers.

CONTENTS

PREFACE

This book is written for deer hunters of all ages and degrees of hunting skill. In close to four decades, I've hunted whitetails with many good partners. From all of them, I've learned something worthwhile to pass on "for the good of the order."

I've attempted to cover all the basics of whitetail hunting and then go beyond those fundamentals. The first thing one learns in writing a book is that, despite all the space that seems to be available, there's still not enough room to say everything about a complex and fascinating subject such as hunting the whitetail. I've omitted archery hunting, for example. That's not out of any personal disapproval of bowhunting. It's a great sport that I enjoyed for years until I came to the reluctant realization that I didn't have time for all the recreation that appeals to me. Rather, the problem is that bowhunting in itself is too complex a subject to do justice to without practically writing a parallel book. I do point out to archers that some of this book's material is still applicable to the bowhunter's pursuit of the wily whitetail.

Although I've hunted a lot of good whitetail country from the Great Lakes states to the Pacific Northwest, no man in a lifetime could thoroughly learn everything about all the regions of the U.S. where whitetails are found. Nonetheless, the whitetail deer's basic habits and mentality don't vary that much from region to region.

Whitetails have given me the slip (and always the thrill) in the mountains of eastern Washington, as well as in Wisconsin's North Woods, Ontario or Oklahoma's Kiamichi country.

The whitetail's challenge as a game animal is the set of defenses and stratagems he has and uses well. He keeps this basic set of tools with him regardless of where he makes his home. Thus, what I've written about whitetail behavior in the West or Midwest readily applies to the same flag-tailed gent in the South's canebrakes and piney woods or in the timbered hills of New England. The most fundamental rule of whitetail hunting always applies everywhere—never underestimate our mutual friend Mr. Buck!

Norm Nelson
Federal Way, Washington

1

The Deer and the People

The buck was splendid when he stepped out of the timber onto the overgrown logging road and stared at the awestruck boy lugging a single-shot grouse gun.

I was that boy, many years ago, and that was my first woodlands encounter with one of the globe's greatest game animals, the Virginia whitetail deer. It was love at first sight. Only another hunter would know what I mean. And only a few hunter-writers such as Ernest Hemingway and José Ortega y Gasset have been able to describe the mystical relationship between the hunter and the game he loves and loves to hunt.

A fine writer and great guy, John Madson, the pundit of Winchester-Western, writes of Americans and the whitetail:

"America grew up eating venison and wearing buckskin.

"We were weaned as a nation on deer meat, took our first toddling steps in deerhide moccasins, and came of age at King's Mountain and New Orleans when our deer-trained riflemen cut down foreign regulars in long, scarlet swaths.

"We scraped, oiled, and stretched buckskin over cabin windows in lieu of glass. When the crops were put by, maybe we walked down the mountain to a turnpike tavern and swapped deer hides for the venomous rum we called 'The Crown's Revenge.' In early Kaintuck when there was no flour, we gave our babies boiled veni-

The whitetail deer, one of the great big-game animals of the world, is highly adaptable to different habitats and is crafty under hunting pressure.

son instead of bread. Moving west, we spliced the first telegraph lines with buckskin thongs and tipped our 30-foot bullwhips with buckskin poppers. We dressed our heroes in buckskin shirts, gloves, or mukluks and sent them off to Lundy's Lane, the Alamo, the Little Big Horn, Attu and Aachen.

"And we're still the People of the Deer. A pair of wealthy Detroit executives, lunching at their club, grin like boys as they plan the fall deer hunt. A Carolina mountain farmer, waking to find frost in the laurel thickets, oils the lock of his 10-pound 'hawg rifle' and winks at his son." *

SUBSPECIES AND SIZES

Named for the new colony where Elizabethan colonists first observed it, the Virginia whitetail deer would be better called the American whitetail. It's found in all of the contiguous 48 states, eight provinces of Canada and ranges down to tropical Central America.

Biologists today say there are 30 subspecies of the basic *Odocoileus virginianus,* as the somewhat clumsy scientific handle goes. Each subspecies bears the *O. v.* name tag, followed by another Latin name. *O. v. dacotensis,* for example, is a Great Plains whitetail named for the Dakotas.

More important to the hunter than a list of subspecies is this general fact: Nature tends to create bigger animals of a given species in the northern range of that species. It's a body heat and energy conservation trick. Northern whitetails typically can be four times the size of the little Florida Keys deer *(O. v. clavium),* which stands about two feet at the shoulder and runs 45 to 60 pounds. The tropical whitetails of lower Mexico, Guatemala and Panama are also little.

How big do whitetails get? That's a fascinating question. In body weight, the biggest whitetail I've ever read of from a reliable source (Minnesota Division of Game and Fish) was a 402-pounder shot by Carl J. Lenander in northern Minnesota in 1926. Game biologists, using the well-established Hornaday formula for converting dressed

---

* From "The White-Tailed Deer," copyright 1961, Olin Mathieson Chemical Corporation. Used by permission.

3

weight into likely live weight, figure that that buck weighed a minimum of 511 pounds when alive—which is the size of many young bull elk. But like a lot of big whitetails from the glaciated soils of the North, which lack lime and calcium, Lenander's trophy did not have a particularly big rack.

Some other records of physically big deer include one cited in 1896 by the great artist-naturalist, Ernest Thompson Seton. That deer, which came from Warren County, New York, weighed 318 pounds dressed, or about 404 pounds calculated live weight. A Michigan buck reported by *Forest & Stream* in 1920 was vouchsafed by witnesses and a set of commercial scales at 354 pounds dressed or a calculated 450 pounds on the hoof. Maine hunter Horace Hinkley in 1955 took a 16-pointer (eastern count) that weighed 355 pounds dressed. A state Department of Game employee calculated the live weight at 488 pounds. Hinkley thinks that estimate was high and, in conservative Maine fashion, believes he'll personally hold still for "well above 450."

The problem in determining the "biggest buck on record" is that no one ever conveniently shoots these monsters next to a set of certifiable scales. A lot of weight is lost in blood and innards when the deer is dressed at the kill scene. Further dehydration in a few days before weighing can rob more weight.

The Hornaday formula converts dressed weight into live weight by adding five ciphers to dressed weight and dividing by 78612. Dressed weight represents .78612 of live weight.

The only standard way of scoring whitetails is the well-known Boone & Crockett Club records, kept by the National Rifle Association. In the appendix of this book are score-sheet reproductions for B & C recording and related information. Boone & Crockett goes by antler size, based on a complex system of measurements and a division into "typical" and "non-typical" types of antlers.

What's at the top of the list? First place for typical whitetail antlers, at a score of 206⅝, goes to a head owned by Charles T. Arnold. The stunning rack was taken by James Jordan, 1914, along Yellow River near Danbury, Wisconsin. To roughly compare with your best fireplace antlers, the Arnold rack has right and left beams each measuring 30 inches, an inside spread of 20⅛ inches and a total of 10 points.

The best non-typical head is a remarkable 49-pointer scoring 286, taken near Brady, Texas, by one Jeff Benson in 1892. Presently

Is Carl Lenander's 1926 whitetail, estimated by the Minnesota Game Department to have had a live weight of 511 pounds, the biggest on record? Lenander was a big man, but the buck (dressed weight 402 pounds) dwarfs him. (PHOTO COURTESY OF MINN. DEPT. OF NATURAL RESOURCES.)

owned by the Lone Star Brewing Company, the head is one of the freak antler developments that can occur in whitetails for a variety of reasons. It looks as if the deer snagged a bunch of petrified rags on his antlers.

Although northern whitetails would hold all unofficial honors for size, significantly many of the heads in the Boone & Crockett records are from all parts of the United States, including the South where deer body sizes are smaller.

Roughly speaking, Seton's rule is probably valid. He said that the average buck from Virginia would weigh about 150 pounds (alive), while the average doe would weigh about 100 pounds. Northward, he added, these weights may be doubled (although I suspect 200-pound does are as unlikely as feathers in a cuckoo clock), while southward, weights would run a third less.

THE ADAPTABLE WHITETAIL

The qualities that make the whitetail a great game animal go beyond sizes. First, the whitetail is wide-ranging and adaptable. Whitetails have done a marvelous job of fitting in with the changes of civilization in North America. The whitetail can live in an untouched wilderness, or he can adapt to suburbia. In fact, he may thrive better in the latter, given a little bedding cover between feeding forays, than in the classic forest primeval.

Second, the whitetail is prolific. Except for two minor and federally protected subspecies, the Columbian whitetail of the coastal Northwest and the Keys deer, whitetail populations are flourishing today as never before. Game managers like to point with pride to the widespread and numerous whitetails in every state today. Although much of this is due to the whitetail itself, a lot of this success is based on good game management.

Actually, we don't know how many whitetails existed in pre-Columbian America. Seton estimated 40 million, but that's a very wild guess. Seton based it on Henry Howe's "Historical Collections of Ohio," which reported a single day's gang hunt in a Medina, Ohio, township of 25 square miles. The hunt allegedly produced 300 deer, plus 17 wolves, 21 bears and other game. That's 12 deer taken per square mile. Seton assumed the hunters couldn't have gotten them all and that there may have been 20 deer per square mile. Seton then marvelously extrapolated this guesswork into an estimated 2 million square miles of North American whitetail range, another guesswork figure of his, and came up with a primitive population of 40 million deer.

Medina township in 1818 may well have supported a high figure of 20 whitetails per square mile. By then there were plenty of thriving pioneer farms scattered throughout substantial hardwood forests—which is a good situation for deer. Seton erred in blithely assuming that this situation was true in the rest of North America. In reality much of the untouched country was very poor whitetail range. Unbroken conifer forests in the North fed and contained few deer. A great deal of the South's primitive forest consisted of pinelands containing little deer browse. The southern hardwoods tended to come in later, after logging and fires removed much of the pine "climax forest."

Wildlife biologists, armed with stronger data than Seton's, are convinced that today's estimated population of 12 million whitetails in the United States is probably much higher than what existed before the white man. But before this happy state of affairs came about, whitetails fell on evil days. In early America, whitetails were four-legged food banks for a pioneer-agrarian population that often had no other source of fresh meat. As the country filled up, relentless meat hunting with dogs, guns and snares either wiped out or reduced to remnants the whitetails of most of the East, South, New England and Midwest. By 1885 only an estimated 350,000 whitetails were left south of Canada.

This was *not* sport hunting but the persistent exploitation of the whitetail for food. While rural residents and commercial market hunters raced each other to shoot what was left, actual sportsmen stood by wringing their hands and saying, "There oughta be a law."

Gradually, their pressures began to result in just such laws. Market hunting was knocked out. Hunting seasons were established, and limits were placed on the number of deer an individual could take in a season. Sportsmen's license money flowed in to finance the beginnings of fairly effective game-law enforcement.

In the early 20th century, the tide was turning. What whitetails remained began repopulating their areas. Regions without deer were restocked by hunter-financed conservation programs or by sportsmen-volunteers themselves. Here, the astonishing fertility of the whitetail as a biological organism came into play. One doe can

7

account for almost two dozen progeny in five years or about 130 in 10 years. Well-fed whitetail does will breed in their first autumn and have fawns on the mothers' birthdays. If does have good diets, a high rate of twin births also occurs, which balloons a herd's numbers even faster. American naturalist George Shiras III pointed out many years ago that two dozen does have the reproductive potential for 3,000 ultimate descendants in 10 years.

About when the turn-of-the-century conservation movement was zeroing in on deer protection and restoration, some other man-made factors were taking place that had a marked effect on whitetails. A combination of logging and wildfires was opening up vast tracts of old-growth evergreen forests, North and South. Previously, these natural forests had overtopping canopy shade that held little deer browse. When the big timber went, the brush species exploded in the newfound sunlight. The deer dependent on such brush for food exploded, too. Areas such as Michigan's Upper Peninsula, northern Minnesota and much of Ontario historically had few deer. In a short span of a few years, whitetails irrupted there, to use the right biological verb.

The 1920s and even into the 1930s was the Golden Age of forest whitetail hunting in much of the U.S. While deer were still recovering from the old meat-hunting wipe-out of the 1800s in eastern and midwestern America's farm country, their populations burst the biological seams in the northern "cutover country." It's significant that a couple of the giant whitetail bucks on record, Minnesota's 500-pounder and New York State's 400-pounder, were taken in second-growth forest zones logged or burned not many years before. Much of Minnesota's Cook County, where Carl Lenander in 1926 took what's apparently the all-time biggest buck on record, was fabulous cut-over deer country then. Today it's some of the poorest deer range, because the forests have grown up again to repeat the cycle of shading out the undergrowth deer need to survive.

The ups and downs of American whitetail herds get to be a complicated story from that point on. In terms of legal protection, the battle was won. Actually it was won too well. Generations of American deer hunters have grown up with the mistaken belief that, if anything, deer should be cautiously underhunted to avoid depleting the resource.

The modern whitetail's biggest enemy is another whitetail. When

8

Minnesota game managers examine some satisfactorily dense browse growing up in an area that was logged and bulldozed specifically for rehabilitation of whitetail-deer range. But such techniques are too expensive per acre to be applied over large areas to keep excess deer populations from starving sooner or later.

forest deer populations took off in the 20th century, severe over-browsing soon began. Also, the cutover and burned forest began to grow new timber stands, repeating the brush shade-out cycle. Increasing deer numbers and decreasing food supplies have mass starvation as a result. Balancing deer populations with food supplies is consequently the key to all management of this species. Today's game managers know this. The problem, as always, is money. Artificial feeding is too costly, impossible over big areas, and can actually cause more problems than it solves. Artificially rehabilitating over-mature forests solely for deer survival is too expensive to do on a large scale. Controlled burning is no cure-all, since it's too expensive in its own right.

Commercial logging, where economically feasible, is the best available deer-management technique. But logging is a matter of hard economics, too, and not enough of it can be done in some of the areas where deer need it the most. When I asked an outstanding American game manager, Milt Stenlund, what his north-country Minnesota region needed to bring deer back to their levels of a couple decades ago, he sadly smiled and said, "About three more wood-pulp mills here would do it nicely."

Even so, the general whitetail deer picture is good in the United States. In our lifetime, deer have come back strongly in the eastern and midwestern farm regions where they were annihilated generations ago. Texas, where commercial grazing and subsistence hunting once wiped out whitetails in large areas, now has an amazing 3.5 million whitetails, largest herd in the nation. States such as Kansas, where deer were unknown for decades, now have enough to support substantial and regular seasons. Oklahoma is seldom thought of as a deer state, but Sooner hunters had a record harvest of 11,548 whitetails in 1976, a 19 percent increase over the previous year.

LET'S GO HUNTING

Why do people love to hunt deer today? As with mountain climbing, for the challenge. The whitetail's greatest virtue as a game animal is more than his wide range, high reproductivity and superb eating qualities. Rather, it's the very difficulty of bagging

10

Basically a homebody, the whitetail doesn't stray far from normal haunts that offer both food and plenty of cover.

him that endears him to all of us who plan, sweat, swear, freeze, and weep over deer hunting.

The whitetail has a distinct personality. He's one of the greatest con artists of all times who lives by the rule (aimed at us) of: "Never give a sucker an even break." Clever, shifty, sneaky are all adjectives that fit him. He's paradoxically shy and curious. He's basically a homebody who sticks within a given territory, unlike some of his migratory mule deer cousins. He uses that territory wonderfully well to evade and confuse the best of hunters. Hunted in fair chase, he's more than a match for most of us most of the time. He has fantastic hearing, a radar-like nose and better eyesight for any movement than we commonly realize.

The whitetail as a mature buck is usually an intelligent pessimist, thoroughly dedicated to keeping his hide intact. The most famous example of how good he is at self-preservation is the test, done years ago, where 39 Michigan deer, nine of them bucks, were stocked in a mile-square enclosure consisting of hardwoods, pine swamps and open pine barrens. Six experienced hunters were turned loose with ideal tracking snow and good weather conditions. It was almost four days before one of them even *saw* a buck. The man-hours to take a buck averaged 51 . . . . and these were reportedly good, canny hunters, at that.

All of these things make the whitetail a most fascinating foe.

2

Good Garb for the Game

Before arming himself or anything else, the whitetail hunter must first get dressed. Unfortunately, a lot of well-intended deer hunts go down the tube right at this fundamental step.

REQUIREMENTS FOR HUNTING CLOTHES

Clothing for deer hunting must be picked on three requirements. First is safety, which includes not only common sense coloration but adhering to the laws of the state you're hunting in. Some states require blaze orange in varying degrees, and others don't. One Canadian province, I am told, required deer hunters to wear white, a color considered a highly dangerous no-no for U.S. hunters. *Quien sabe?*

The second requirement is that the duds you wear must do the job of keeping you comfortable in the outdoors environment you'll be operating in. That means protection from chilling, overheating and moisture.

The third requirement is that hunting clothes and footwear ideally should not add to the problem of hunter movement noise. This, as we shall see, is a real challenge.

13

Safety

Decades ago, when deer woods began to get a bit crowded by our grandsires (who didn't know what crowding really was), state legislatures or game commissions started requiring some red to be worn by hunters. It was a hip-shot, unscientific opinion. Red is not a good safety color. In certain light conditions, it can look brown or black.

The big upsurge in hunting—and hunting accidents—after World War II brought the protective safety color problem to the fore again. Experts pointed out the shortcomings of red. Yellow was experimented with. Lighter in tone than red, it stands out more brightly under poor light conditions. The problem with yellow is that it can appear white at times.

The next step was orange. It's the best compromise, particularly when served up as a bright, fluorescent orange made possible through modern chemistry. But only recently has it been possible to dye wool in fluorescent colors.

Wool is far and away the answer to the deer hunter's textile prayer. It's warm when dry, water-repellent, fairly tough (depending upon weight and weave), and it manages to hold some heat even when wet. Above all, it's a quiet fabric to wear in the woods.

Quiet clothing is vital, for reasons we shall see in Chapter 14. Cotton and nylon fabrics and vinyl-coated raingear are noisy when brushed against twigs or even when just flexing against itself while the wearer is in motion.

Comfort and Noise

Most deer hunting in the United States is done in autumnal climates that are at least pretty cool part of the time and lethally arctic-like in some northern zones. Even the deer hunter in the Deep South has to dress warmly on those frosty mornings that the lyrics of "Dixie" mention in passing. The hunter in the north has to dress warmly not just for comfort but to stay alive.

Our deer-hunting forefathers didn't worry too much about deer-hunting clothes. First, they were naturally tougher folks. The majority of them lived in rural environments, worked outdoors, lacked central heating, and survived trips to the outhouse at 20° below zero. Second, relatively few of them could afford clothes intended

Wool outer garments are the only practical hunting clothes for hunting in wet or snowy weather like this. Footwear should be both surefooted and waterproof.

When working through typical brush conditions like this, the forest whitetail hunter should wear outer clothing that will make as little noise as possible.

just for hunting. They made do with the wool mackinaws or sheep-skin coats they normally wore for cold-weather work outdoors.

After World War II, consumer affluence saw outdoorsmen going in for better cold-weather garb, such as down garments and insulated rubber boots. Fishnet underwear, something we learned about from the German army (which allegedly picked it up from Norwegian fishermen), made its appearance. So did down booties, insulated Korean War boots, and even electrically heated socks.

If all this sounds complicated and expensive, don't worry. The two basic rules in dressing up for a deer-hunting soiree are: Stick with wool for quietness in the brush, and dress in layers. Let's take a typical example.

It's before dawn on a chilly November morning, with the temperature in the low 20s or upper teens. You're planning to slip out on a stand for the first hour of daybreak. After that, you and the others will be making some drives. Part of the time you'll be playing dog on the drive; at other times, you'll be a stander. A peek outside shows stars—clear day coming up. That means it will warm up by about 10 a.m. It won't be a hot day, but it will be warm enough to make you awfully hot and sweaty on a drive if you're overdressed. Actually, by midday it will be warm enough to wear only a wool shirt and no jacket, at least while you're moving on the drive.

But you've got to wear something warmer early in the day, or you'll freeze while standing or sitting motionless for an hour or so at dawn.

My personal solution for these potential problems of being too cold and/or too warm in the same hour is to start with a pair of cotton thermal longjohns. Over those go a pair of medium-weight soft wool trousers, held by a sturdy leather belt, not suspenders. (Suspenders are too much of a nuisance when you must answer Nature's major call.) On top, I'll wear a cotton T-shirt, a light-weight red or orange flannel shirt and a red medium-weight wool shirt. Then I'll slip on a blaze-orange down vest and top the whole works with a medium-weight wool hunting jacket. If law requires it, a blaze-orange plastic vest is worn outside the main jacket.

This garb will keep me warm in the chilly dawn temperature range for an hour or so. Later, when the sun is up, the day is warming, and I'm facing a foot drive through some heavy going, the down vest and medium wool shirt will be removed, rolled up, and stashed in the rear game pocket of my main jacket. (If your deer-hunting jacket lacks an inside rear game pocket, prevail on some nice lady with a sewing machine to install one . . . no big problem. But don't make it of nylon because of that fabric's noisy swishiness.)

If the day promises rain or snow, I'll pack a light but durable blaze-orange rain jacket, hip-length, in my gamebag pocket. But I'll put it on only if a major wetting is in the making, because such rain garments are awfully noisy to wear in the brush. Ponchos or longer parkas pose noise and movement problems except for a hunter on the stand.

In colder weather, the same layered principle applies, only with more layers and heavier stuff. Hunting in my native northern Minnesota, I've sat out on a deer stand for two mortal hours on a morning when the camp thermometer showed 22° below zero, fortunately without wind. In such weather, a hunter could use fishnet underwear, two-piece blended wool underwear, heavier wool pants, two wool shirts in lieu of one flannel and one wool, a down jacket under his outer wool jacket, and a good wool scarf as a heat gasket.

Even in zero cold, a hunter can still get overheated when moving through tough going or dragging out a deer. Be prepared to remove some of the garments then. If you work up a sweat in cold weather, then you're really going to get cold the next time you stand still for any length of time or if a wind comes up.

The temptation for the northern hunter is to buy a very heavy outer jacket or down parka for those near-arctic cold snaps. The problem is that such garments are a burden if you start working up lots of body heat while on the move. Once you take off such a heavy outer garment, there's also the problem of what to do with it. A daypack is one solution. But it's better to stick with the multi-layer principle and take off easily-stowed inner garments as necessary.

The best hunting headwear again is wool for quietness. Good wool hunting caps are hard to find these days. They've been replaced by mouton-trimmed plastic abominations that are too warm and too noisy on the move. A wool or acrylic watch cap is warm enough for most deer hunting and easily stuffs in a pocket when you want to quickly cool your body. The big network of arteries and veins in your neck, face and scalp make a dandy radiator for quickly "dumping" excess body heat. By the same token, warm headgear in place helps retain body heat. Veteran mountain climbers have an old rule: "If your feet are cold, first put your cap

17

Cold-weather deer hunting requires intelligent choices of multi-layered clothes, particularly for long waits in windy tree stands, as this hunter is doing.

back on." But the problem with a watch cap is the lack of a sun-shading bill or visor.

A hunting cap should also have some sort of ear flaps, since ears are easily frostbitten. A parka hood is good ear protection but tends to muffle your hearing—or drown it out with hood fabric rustle.

Gloves give finger mobility but may not be warm enough in really cold weather. Mitts are warm but obviously impossible to fire a gun with. Mitts with slotted palms to allow fingers out for gun operation are not suitable for fast shooting. Better is a mitt with a separate index finger.

On the move, I'll stick with a glove on my shooting hand, although I may wear a mitt at the same time on my left hand. I remember all too well a horror story involving a parallel still hunt I was doing with my uncle Ralph. Without seeing it, I jumped a big buck. With a snort and a rush, he went crashing through dense white cedar cover to my right where Ralph was, and I waited confidently for the shot.

None came. Turns out the deer came boiling out of the cedars and almost ran over Ralph—who at that time was frantically trying to shuck a heavy leather chopper mitt with a wool liner in order to get off a shot. By the time the mitt was off, the buck was gone. Opportunities like that in timber cover can be measured in seconds.

The layered principle works as well on gloves as it does on your body. A light liner glove of rayon, thermal-weave cotton or light wool, covered by a heavier wool glove, is good for zero weather. If you're going to be on stand in such weather, pack a pair of mitts along. A stander usually has time enough to slip off a loose mitt.

One warning: If you like to fiddle with a rifle's adjustable trigger to get a light, crisp pull desired by marksmen, don't set it too light for gloved use in cold weather, or a premature shot can occur before your sights are fairly on the target. And don't open any old mental wounds by asking me how I know.

Warm-weather deer-hunting clothes are simple—wear what's legal and comfortable. This may well rule out wool, of course. The usual substitute in warm weather is denim in trousers. Unfortunately, new denim can be stiff and noisy. An old pair of jeans, repeatedly laundered into supple, quiet softness, is the best choice by far if you can't wear soft wool. A lightweight flannel shirt is quiet and wearable unless it really gets hot. Then, a T-shirt of the correct legal color in your state may be the best top garment. But it may be

19

smart to have some warmer clothes in car, camp, or daypack if the warm weather turns cold or wet.

FOOTWEAR

Hunting footwear is a complex subject. The right boots are a vital part of the deer hunter's ensemble. Or, to put it the other way, the wrong boots can prematurely end his hunt because his half-frozen, wet feet can't take it any more. Improper footwear can even be dangerous in steep country and slippery going.

The great standby for millions of deer hunters has been the rubber shoepack with leather uppers. For all-around use except in dry, rocky country, such footwear is still the best. Two basic types are available. One has a sharp-edged, tough rubber sole with heavy cleating molded in. Sorel, a Canadian bootery firm, is a prominent maker of these, exporting them widely in the States. The other type usually has softer rubber, rounded edges on the sole and only a modicum of tread . . . which usually wears off in a couple of seasons anyway.

If you hunt hilly country, pick the sharp-edged, deep-lug shoepacks for traction. They're noisier and heavier, alas, but they will keep you from breaking a leg better than the quieter but slippery round-sole shoepacks.

Another alternative is the all-rubber boot. These are more waterproof than shoepacks but don't provide as much ankle support. They can be had in insulated models that are somewhat warmer than the standard rubber models.

Any boot's cold-weather protection depends heavily upon good felt insoles and the right kind of socks. If you hunt a cold climate and particularly if you spend lots of time on stand, buy boots a full size too large to allow room for a thick felt insole and two pairs of heavy wool socks. Every night in camp, hang these, insoles included, to dry. During the day, they become damp from foot perspiration.

A great system for the sub-arctic weather that northern state and Canadian deer hunters often endure consists of oversize shoepacks with full felt-liner boots inside. This combo is warmer than any foam-insulated "Korean" boot I've tried yet.

So far I've avoided leather boots. The reason is that I've found

20

leather hunting boots useful only in warm, dry weather. If you hunt deer in Arizona or Texas, for example, good leather boots are excellent. In cold, wet climes, they are not worth a damn. A porous material, leather cannot be truly waterproofed, particularly when the boot is made of stitched segments. And don't be misled by ad claims. Militant consumerism is not my dish; but I must blow the whistle on some fairly expensive leather boots such as Herman Survivors, which are advertised to be waterproof and in my experience most assuredly have not been waterproof. In marshy country or snow, rubber footwear (which includes leather-topped packs) is the only way to go if the weather is at all chilly. Cold, wet feet are second only to a first-class toothache for ruining a day of deer hunting.

But some whitetail hunting doesn't require the warmth and moisture protection of rubber boots. Shoepacks would be miserable in the warm weather of the Texas hill country or in Wyoming in October, when temperatures can be in the 80s. A moderately lightweight leather boot with decent lug soles is best for all-around use, which probably involves some hills. If flat terrain is your invariable hunting country, skip the lug soles and go for crepe-soled bird-hunting boots for quietness.

In the last generation or two, boots have shrunk—downward, that is. In early days, hunters were sore afflicted with high-laced boots that covered most of the calf. The only thing these are good for is riding a horse. They're miserable for the foot hunter, because the high upper either cramps blood circulation if tightly laced or chafes heck out of the calf if not tightly laced. A boot with an upper measuring about 12 inches from ground level is much more practical. Snow entry can be best blocked by internally blousing the cuffs of the trousers, military style, or simply tying spare laces or nylon cord around them on the outside.

A word on boot care. Good leather boots need maintenance. In dry, dusty use, take the trouble to clean them at times with a damp cloth and saddle soap to remove the abrasive dirt that otherwise is minutely sawing through the leather fibers on every step. Apply oil or boot grease only to dry leather. Never force-dry leather with close-up heat. This fries the internal leather oils right out, causing very rapid cracking and failure of the fibers.

Rubber boots are vulnerable to tears or punctures. Running into old barbed wire on the ground is a great way to do this. Hot patch materials from the tire store or auto-parts shop is the surest way of repairing these, although black rubber cement will serve temporarily in a pinch. Store rubber boots in a cool place between seasons—heat and direct sunlight will harm the rubber.

A final but important word on footwear. Get rid of leather bootlaces and replace them with good nylon laces. These can be tightened enough for proper ankle support. Rawhide laces stretch when wet and lose strength in the bargain, often breaking when you try to cinch them up.

In summary on the matter of clothing, first be sure your outer garments match your state's legal color requirements. For cold weather use, dress in layers. Learn to match your clothes and footwear to the kind of hunting you do in your climate. Experience will soon show you how to fine-tune your choice of hunting duds beyond the basics.

3

Best Bets for Brush Guns

The first argument about the ideal North American deer-hunting weapon started when the first Spanish conquistador pot-shot a whitetail with a matchlock. Probably the venison wasn't even dressed before some companion was criticizing the shooter's powder charge—or second-guessing that a crossbow or wheel lock would have done a better job.

I once had a deer-hunting neighbor (with a ballistics engineering background, no less) who swore by a Winchester .458 Magnum in the Model 70 African. This, he declared, punched through more puckerbush with less bullet deflection than any other bullet size and laid out a deer faster with less blood-shot meat. In between the muzzleloader and my chum's literal elephant gun, American hunters over the centuries have used everything from .22 rimfires to high-velocity modern magnums. And everyone still argues about what makes the best whitetail gun.

The answer is obvious. The best whitetail gun is the one that does the best job for you. That can depend upon a number of factors.

Shooter capability is one. This includes a combination of marksmanship skill and recoil tolerance. Strength and willingness of the individual shooter also determine how heavy a gun he or she can and will wrestle through brush all day.

THREE CATEGORIES OF WHITETAIL RIFLES

Your own mode of hunting is the most important factor in deciding what's the best whitetail gun. Basically, deer rifles fall into three major categories. First is the "brush gun" for use at close range in heavy cover. Ideally, a brush gun should be fairly light, short for ease of handling in thickets, and carry a sighting system for close work—iron sights or low-power scope.

Second is a relatively new classification of deer rifle. Call it not just a rifle but an actual weapons system for specialized long-distance shooting. Historically, whitetails have not usually been taken at long distances. But certain factors are giving rise to new opportunities here, to be explained in a later chapter.

In a third category are compromise guns that will do an adequate job either as true forest rifles or for longer-range work. As with any compromise, performance won't be ideal in either end of the spectrum. But call this category a good, all-around rifle choice. Long-range rifles and compromise rifles will be covered in the next chapter.

A brush gun need not be a highly accurate weapon. Once I was assisting hunters who were sighting-in at a public range before deer season. One chap shambled up with a battered .401 Winchester self-loader. The rifling was so bad in this relic that the bullets were keyholing (hitting sideways) at random on a large target sheet at 50 yards.

"That's good enough," he drawled. And it was. I later learned that he got a deer at about 30 yards, which is a fairly typical range for taking deer in dense forest cover. Minnesota, a forest-whitetail state, ran a deer-hunting survey and found that the average shooting range of hunters who scored the previous season was 27 yards.

Speed of repeat fire is the most debated point in all deer gun arguments. It's also the most misunderstood factor.

A good percentage of deer taken in close-range forest conditions are on the run, jumped by the shooter, or running from some other hunter's approach. Briefly, the best way to hit a deer running broadside or tangentially in heavy cover is to rapidly find a clear hole in the intervening brush somewhere ahead of the game. Cover that and shoot as the deer flashes through it.

All this is very fast work, on a par with quail or ruffed-grouse shooting. The judgment and eye-hand coordination capacities of your brain are being called upon to do some split-second functioning with a high degree of correctness, if you're to have venison liver for supper.

You can't always count on scoring with that first shot, either. The less mechanical fussing around with your rifle action that you have to do between shots while trying to keep an eye on a bounding deer, finding a hole ahead, and lining up on that hole, the better your chances of doing those crucial latter jobs.

The poorest repeater for this work is a bolt action. Why? Because the shooter must do several things. First, he must disengage his finger sideways from the trigger. Then he must grab the bolt knob, which can be awkward contact to make with a wool-gloved hand. After that, he has to lift the bolt, retract it fully, slam it forward and down, remove his hand, put it back on the grip, and then find the trigger again with his index finger.

That's at least seven manual coordination tasks to be done in preparing a bolt gun to shoot again, which is simply too much when contending with fast-running game in heavy cover. Only a single-shot breechloader would be clumsier.

Of course, with hours of dry-firing drill, a shooter *can* work up to an incredible speed in recharging even a Mauser-type bolt action, which is slower and stiffer by its design than the old Lee-Enfields, Krags, or modern, short-lift bolt actions. A shooter I knew was so fast with a Mauser that he could fire a second shot with acceptable hunting-range accuracy before the first empty cartridge hit the deck. It took untold hours of drill to attain that skill. Few hunters would take the effort to achieve it.

But the repeating-rifle problem doesn't involve just speed. It's also a question of how much activity must be done in rearming the gun, since all this serves as a distraction to the brain functions that are frantically trying to solve that problem of finding a hole for a good snapshot. No grouse hunter in his right mind would consider a bolt-action shotgun to be a good partridge arm. By the same token, I'll defy the entire Great American Bolt Action Cult and its editorial establishment by declaring that *for brush hunting only,* a bolt-action rifle is a dismal deer rifle indeed. If most or all of your deer hunting is done in dense timber and brush, you'll be happier with another form of repeater.

25

THE LONG-LIVED LEVER GUNS

If any arm qualifies as the standard American hunting rifle, it's the lever action. Thereby hangs a tale that explains in part why a variety of good lever guns are both popular and available today, despite certain design limitations.

American manhood began its century-plus love affair with the lever repeater during the Civil War, when fast-firing Henry and Spencer repeating carbines were used by some soldiers in the Union cavalry.

Postwar pioneers heading into the West remembered those accounts of how brave waves of Confederates wilted under the bullet storm of Union lever guns. Confidence in his lever gun's equalizing firepower was certainly a main reason why the homesteader of the Western frontier even dared to attempt scattered, single-family homesteading in a land peopled with enemies to whom merciless raider warfare was a way of life.

Fortunately, today's lever gun buyer is getting more than an expensive piece of horse-opera hardware. For forest deer hunting, a light or medium-weight lever-action gun always has been and still remains an extremely useful taker of venison.

For the average deer hunter, a lever-action repeater is better than a turn-bolt gun. But not because it's that much faster in pure speed of fire. The important thing is that working a typical lever gun is far less distracting. For one thing, you're not yanking your right hand on a bolt action's handle back at your right eye, which causes many a hunter to unconsciously flinch his face clean off the stock comb. The quick fore-and-aft throw of a lever gun comes to be an automatic, non-distracting function for the shooter far more easily than all the monkey motion necessary for a bolt gun.

Furthermore, the exposed, clearly visible hammer of a typical lever gun (the "hammerless" Savage 99 and discontinued Winchester 88 excepted) is regarded as a better and faster safety system by many once-a-year, hunting-only shooters. Cocking the hammer is at least as fast or faster than finding and disengaging the somewhat clumsy, long-throw wing safety of the usual bolt-action rifle.

The typical modern lever-action rifle is a short-action, relatively light weapon unless given a long, weighty barrel. For forest hunting, this is no mean virtue. A heavy gun of any action mode is a tiresome burden in thick forest and brush, but a light lever gun such as the classic Model 94 Winchester is a friendly, no-sweat companion. The narrow receiver carries well in one hand (although the unshielded metal is cold in zero-degree weather). The slab-sided slenderness of the typical lever gun makes it the best of all saddle scabbard repeaters for the horseback hunter, too.

There are drawbacks. Some lever gun designs simply can't be chambered for more powerful, modern cartridges. The Winchester 94 is a prime example. It was intended for moderate-performance, rimmed cartridges of the .30–30 class.

The biggest design problem of the 94 series, however, is its unsuitability for scope mounting, since it ejects cartridges straight up. With the Marlin lever guns, the Savage 99, the Browning BLR or the relatively new, classic-styled Mossberg 479, normal scope placement is no problem. But any scope's utility is greatly improved with a higher-comb stock. This should be considered by any hunter who wants to put a scope on his lever gun.

Gun writers for years have been writing off lever rifles as lingering throwbacks. After the big Winchester 71 in .348 caliber was dropped years ago, the keyboard kommandos disparaged the surviving lever line as light deer rifles only, okay for women, kids or adult males who didn't know any better. One of the editorial high priests of the Bolt Action Cult went so far as to predict the lever gun would eventually fade from production.

He couldn't have been more wrong. My dog-eared copy of the 1952 Official Gun Book reveals that 13 lever gun variants made by three manufacturers were available in six different deer-suitable calibers, .25 to .35, that year. By contrast, the market in 1976 offered a surprising 23 lever gun models, suitable for deer hunting, from seven different sources. These include 11 calibers, ranging from .243 to .45–70. Reestablishment of the long-overlooked .358 Winchester in the lever gun line via Browning's fine BLR model and the Savage 99 provides energy in about the .30–06 class.

Remember what I said about historic glamour? Seven of the 23 lever guns on the market at the time of America's Bicentennial are duplicates of the long-vanished Winchester '66 "Yellow Boy" and Winchester '73 models that really won the West. Since these are primarily historical replicas, perhaps few are sold for actual hunting use. Considering the current blackpowder craze, however, you can never tell.

Not just historical replicas, but up-to-date lever guns are also bought for their subconscious historical associations. The man laying hands on a lever action is fondling *the* classic American rifle. He's in touch with a tradition that starts with cavalry battles in the Shenandoah and at Beecher's Island, goes through young Teddy Roosevelt's hunting days in the Badlands, and ends up in dim, boyhood memories of well-oiled, octagon-barreled lever guns in dad's or granddad's closet corner.

Unlike the gun writer who predicted the eventual demise of the lever-action gun after World War II, I'll make an opposite forecast. The lever action will be made and sold just as long as Americans keep their freedom to bear arms. The lever guns are both fine deer rifles and an indissoluble tie with a time that made us a nation.

PUMPS AND AUTOLOADERS

Pumps and autoloaders are even better snapshooting rifles in timber than lever guns. The pump action involves the minimum of manual distraction for the harried shooter trying to find his hypothetical whitetail hole in the alders. The autoloader, obviously, requires no repeat shot distraction at all.

In early days, autoloaders were considered unsafe by some wagging graybeards. The theory was that any hunter with an autoloader would hose out such a volume of lead that he'd gun down hunting buddies and innocent bystanders with wild abandon.

That, of course, is a ridiculous assumption that has never been substantiated in any safety study. My own conviction is that when swinging his gun on a running deer, a hunter with the least reloading distraction is the most likely to spot another redcoat in a potential line of fire. The autoloader might well be the safest deer rifle from this standpoint, although all such hypotheses are highly theoretical. Suffice it to say that while autoloaders have soared in use in recent decades, the statistical rate of deer-hunting gun mishaps has been declining, which disproves the anti-autoloader view.

Despite American hunters' enduring fondness for pump shotguns, surprisingly few pump rifles in big-game calibers have adorned sporting-goods store counters.

Two of these that many oldsters will recall were the Remington 14 and succeeding 141 Gamemaster series. They were short-action jobs, made for the rimless Remington equivalents of general .30–30 class cartridges. Remington killed off the 141 in 1950. It was happily succeeded in 1952 by a great woods rifle, the 760 pump action, also called the Gamemaster.

This is a versatile rifle, noted for the kind of accuracy once expected only from bolt guns. The strong, multiple front-locking lugs of the 760 make it possible for Remington to produce 760's in a host of potent calibers, of which the .30–06 has been the star performer on the market.

The only other trombone-action big-game rifle made today is the relatively new Savage 170 slide action. Running a half-pound lighter than a 760 of the same barrel length, the 170 is chambered only for the .30–30.

We now move into the cussed and discussed field of autoloading deer rifles and what they can do for the hungry hunter of the wily whitetail. Two oldies, the Winchester 07 and the renowned, Browning-design Remington 8/81, are no longer with us. The post-World War II era of the autoloader began with Remington's 740, chambered for high-performance cartridges including the .30–06. The 740 was not very accurate, however. A chum of mine drove himself to distraction trying to find loads, handmade or factory, that would group in his new, scoped 740 some 20 years ago. Four inches at 100 yards was the best it could do, nor was he alone among 740 owners in his anguish.

That's sufficient accuracy for much forest deer hunting, but Remington wisely designed the barrel bedding problems out of the 740 and called the new version the 742. The 742 turned out to be a reasonably accurate, reliable, successful autoloader.

In the 1950s Winchester brought out an autoloader called the 100. It lasted a few years and was dropped, despite a good reputation among hunters. The longest round that the Model 100's short action could take was the Winchester .308, a cutdown version of the '06 and a fine deer cartridge.

Three more autoloaders came on the market in recent years: the small Ruger .44 Magnum carbine, firing a big pistol cartridge adequate for close-up whitetails; the little-known Harrington & Richardson 360 Ultra Auto in .243 and .308; and the interesting Browning BAR. The last includes two lines, one using standard big-game cartridges to .30–06, the other chambered for big, belted magnums. In addition, several military style, gas-operated autoloaders are available in .308, including the American Armalite Mark IV Sport-

One of the author's favorite whitetail rifles is this delightfully handy Winchester Model 55 in .30-30 caliber. A variant of the Model 94, this gun was a straight-grip predecessor of the Winchester 64.

Forest-country whitetail hunters often like shorter rifles. Al Nelson, author's brother, favors this 18-inch-barrel bolt-action carbine.

This whitetail hunter's late-model Marlin 336 lever gun in .30-30 (.30 WCF) with a good 2½X scope is an up-to-date version of the classic deer rifle for timber hunting.

N. E. Nelson, the author's father, here packs a venerable long-barrelled version of the classic Winchester Model 94. In various hands, this rifle has accounted for scores of deer in half a century of use in typical dense-timbered whitetail habitat such as this.

er. The latter firearm is ugly as sin and looks too much like something out of "Star Wars" to ever appeal to traditionalist hunters.

WOODS CARTRIDGE CHOICES

Reviewing the whole lineup of lever, pump and autoloading rifles suitable for whitetail hunting in the traditional, dense-woods mode, the American hunter has a bewildering range of choices. Some three dozen rifle models and variants are available. Further complicating the picture are a range of calibers in current-production forest rifles from .243 to .45–70. "Which cartridge" accounts for as much verbal flak among deer hunters as "which rifle."

Heretical as it sounds to gun nuts who've dedicated their lives to learning the litany of ballistics tables, choosing a cartridge for whitetail forest hunting is not a critically tough matter. Any of those currently offered in the .24 to .45 caliber range will adequately reduce well-hit whitetails to possession, as the law puts it, at the ranges almost always encountered in forest hunting. It can be a different matter in some mountain hunting or in working big burns or clearcuts; and this will be covered in the next chapter on long-range rifles and all-around rifles.

A rule of thumb purely for forest hunting is that a decent whitetail cartridge power threshold is a minimum of 1000 foot-pounds of muzzle energy. Don't worry about energy data at 100, 200 or more yards for forest hunting, because you can spend a lifetime of forest-hunting whitetail seasons without getting a shot beyond 50 yards.

The 1000-foot-pound threshold rules out such marginal loads as the ancient .44–40, which is still available, as cited, in replicas. True, an awful lot of venison was piled up by .44–40 and similar loads. For that matter, a lot of black-powder muzzleloading rifles are in that power category. And yes, you can take whitetails with such low-power loads—if you're a marksman who can place his shot in a vital area and enough of a sportsman to not shoot when unsure of lethal bullet placement.

While it's true that poor bullet placement can cost you lost deer even with powerful cartridges, the fact remains that you have more margin for error with husky calibers. I've seen a deer poorly hit with a powerful bullet hump up and freeze in place, allowing a fast coup-de-grace second shot. With a low-power load, such a hit would usually mean a lost cripple, feeding the ravens next day.

Conversely, the arbitrary 1000-foot-pound figure would categorically okay the hotter .22 centerfire varmint loads, from the .222 Remington on up. Yet many states specifically outlaw such cartridges for deer hunting.

I think such laws are basically correct. The .22 hotshots are not good choices for the type of forest deer hunting that's usually done in this country. But I also think that Texas deer hunters who legally use .22 centerfires on whitetails are within the bounds of both sportsmanship and practicality—for *their* circumstances. Some Texas whitetails are smaller than the big, northern subspecies. And a great deal of Texas hunting is done from well-established stands, for standing or walking deer at fairly close ranges. Under those conditions, a .222 or .22–250 will kill effectively and humanely. I once shot a dog-crippled deer for a game warden, using my Remington .222 crow rifle. At 25 yards, the tiny 50-grain bullet blew a tennis ball-sized hole clean through the neck of the whitetail which, you may be sure, never even heard the shot.

But just as with the old black-powder slowpokes, the .22 centerfires don't have any performance margin to forgive a poorly placed hit. The question is moot anyway, as most states don't allow these rifles for deer.

If we dispose of the marginal choices, what should we pick from the more practical forest deer loads? It would be foolish for any writer to lay down a bunch of arbitrary dictates, because the writer cannot possibly know how and where the reader hunts. Even in so-called forest hunting, there are many different kinds of cover situations and hunting modes. I can only tell you what I'd pick for certain, generalized hunting setups.

First, I'd choose the rifle best matched to most of my hunting. If I did a lot of deer stalking in close-range, dense forest, I'd pick a light, fast-handling carbine. Many are available. The .44 Magnum Ruger autoloader would be a dandy, for example. I'm personally fond of my 1894 Marlin (with open iron sights) in this caliber, a six-pound gem that's a pal, not a pain, to carry all day through the shin-tangles. The .44 Magnum's paper ballistics are not hair-raising, even from a carbine in lieu of a pistol barrel. But the big, heavy (240 grain) flatnosed or hollow-point slugs are highly lethal, without the excessive meat pulping of high-velocity rifle loads at close range. A lever gun in .35 Remington is another good alternative. And the old .30–30 liveth yet to do this work well.

More versatility for an occasional long shot would be assured with a more powerful cartridge. In hunting country that offered longer ridge-to-ridge shots, I'd choose a Remington 760 pump in .308 or .30–06 caliber. If deer hunting overlaps chances at bigger stuff, such as elk or moose, a good brush gun choice would be the Savage 99 or Browning BLR lever guns in .358 Winchester. Introduced in 1955 as a necked-up .308, the .358 is a superb forest cartridge, almost totally ignored by velocity-nutty buyers.

Whitetail hunting can include lots of stump-sitting. This usually means deliberate, well-chosen shots at slinking, walking or trotting deer, although sometimes a whitetail spooked by drivers comes by like the Wabash Cannonball making up lost time. Any of the close-range, jump-shooting loads from the .44 Magnum on up will work here, of course. The 6 mm. family in both Remington 6 mm. and Winchester .243 are not ideal brush rifles, but they do well in this kind of stand shooting, where you have the best chance to get off a clean, undeflected shot.

There is one warning regarding whitetail loads. Don't pick too heavy a bullet, designed for bigger game. A classic example is the 220-grain bullet in various ammo makers' .30–06 loadings. These stiff-jacketed elk-bear-moose slugs can rip through a big whitetail without sufficient bullet expansion to do a clean killing job.

BRUSH DEFLECTION AND BULLETS

This brings up the whole unanswered question of brush deflection and bullets. Conventional wisdom has always held that big, slow-moving slugs were less liable to deflect and miss the target. That's not necessarily always true. No one has yet figured out how to reliably run meaningful tests on bullet deflection. Attempts by the scientific method have involved shooting through screens of dowel pegs to assure a "constant" kind of obstruction. These tests are clouded, however, because dry, hardwood dowels are notably different in resilience and tensile strength from green branches in the woods. Even among forest flora, there will be great variations. A bullet that has to smack through some dry pine branehes is facing highly brittle obstructions. The same bullet fired through a clump of tough alder or ironwood brush runs a much different obstacle course.

One thing that seems realistic in brush-deflection tests is that a long, highly stabilized bullet is less prone to deflection than a short bullet fired from fast-twist rifling, which just barely stabilizes it.

Shooting through a real brush screen is a toss-up with any bullet, and a maze of pole-sized young trees is even worse—particularly hardwoods such as birch or maple. Try to avoid such shots and pick a hole instead. As we'll see in a later chapter, this is why a scope helps in forest hunting, even though you don't need the scope's precision to effectively hit a deer at short range.

The inherent problems of shooting in the forest are why many woods hunters prefer bigger calibers and round-nose bullets. Such hunters hope that these combinations will get through brush and limbs better than smaller, pointed bullets. But the best insurance against brush deflection is to avoid desperation shots through such obstacles.

Meanwhile, "I must have hit a twig," remains the classic excuse for all of us when we miss deer in the timber. If Coronado's musketeer missed his first shot at a Texas whitetail, that's probably the excuse he used too.

4

All-Around Deer Rifles

SHOOTING AT LONG RANGE

Although most whitetail weapons are used at short range on this cover-loving game, occasional long shots are offered, primarily in hill or mountain country, East or West. Even flat country can provide long-range whitetail shooting in clearcut logging areas or old forest-fire burns. In the North, muskeg bogs cover some huge areas, broken with islands of black spruce or willow. Deer cross on well-established trails from one timber island to another, and this may require distant shots.

Long-range opportunities on whitetails first occurred some decades ago after the great forest fires of the early 20th century left terrain naked to sunlight, resulting first in an explosion of browse plants, then an explosion of deer populations, as we saw in Chapter 1. Bemused hunters found themselves pecking away at whitetails visible, for once, on distant hillsides. Low-velocity clunkers such as the .38–40 and .38–55 were hopeless for this work, but the .25–35 Winchester and its .25 Remington counterpart were well-suited for it. Velocity of these little 117-grain bullets was not significantly better than the 170-grain slugs of the standard .30–30 and its Remington and Savage peers. However, the .25's "carried out" better, thanks to their superior ballistic coefficient—an index of a bullet's long-range capabilities. But those post-forest-fire clearings soon grew back into standing timber, and the need for longer-range whitetail rifles vanished—until recently.

We no longer permit forest fires on such a large scale. But stepped-up forest management work has caused an increase in clearcutting in the Lakes states, the Northeast, Northwest, South and some parts of the Rocky Mountain region—just about anywhere commercial forests are found, which is much of the United States.

Clearcutting means more deer, and it also means a different way of taking whitetails. To score in such areas, you have to hunt clearcut edges at dusk and dawn to catch night-feeding deer coming or going. Also, deer sometimes bed down in clearcuts, beside concealing logging slash or brush. I once got a telephoto color photo of a nice, three-point buck bedded down in the cool shade of a natural washout under a mammoth stump in a Pacific Northwest clearcut.

Such hunting often requires long-range shots. Arbitrarily I call any deer shot of 300 yards or more a long-range one. Such shooting requires not just thoughtful consideration of a rifle, but a whole weapons system. This means the right rifle (accurate, capable of using high-intensity cartridges); the right choice of cartridge and load (providing relatively flat trajectory with sufficient deer-killing power 'way out yonder); a sighting system (sufficient magnification and optical sharpness, plus the right kind of reticule for precision shooting); *and* a skilled operator capable of using this whole system. All this is a huge jump from the typical brush rifle and its modest aiming system of iron sights or low-power, wide-field scopes.

PICKING A CARTRIDGE

The best way to equip yourself for long-range whitetail hunting is first to pick your cartridge and then find a rifle, appropriate to your pocketbook and tastes, that can use this cartridge. This is a complete flip-flop from the way deer rifles were chosen years ago. Earlier deer hunters tended to pick a rifle based on its action—how the blamed thing fed shells from magazine to chamber—and didn't concern themselves too much about what kind of shells it used, within reasonable limitation.

What makes the best long-range whitetail cartridge? Actually, there's no single "best" one, standing head and shoulders above competitors. Playing the numbers game with the ballistic tables, you find that many high-intensity loads are similar in results at long range. The .30-caliber magnums as a class have little difference. The highly popular 7 mm. Remington Magnum has a slight edge, if any, over the best 150-grain spitzer loads in the non-magnum .270. The .340 Weatherby has little margin over the similar .338 Winchester.

One key factor is how much recoil and muzzle blast the shooter can handle without accuracy being impaired. Any flinching tendency is ruinous to precision marksmanship, as target or varmint shooters will attest.

BOLT ACTIONS—THE PROS AND CONS

Now for the glamour pants of modern sporting rifles—the bolt-action models, in all their somewhat overrated glory. The basic turn-bolt design is an oldie, dating well back into the 19th century. The typical modern bolt gun has a tight-breeching lock-up that allows use of the most powerful cartridges that modern technology will permit.

Actually, that's about all bolt guns have going for them as hunting rifles. Their thick-bodied design is not as nice to carry in one hand as the slender lever guns. Awkward safeties on some bolt guns are a drawback for a fast first shot in the timber. The protuberance of most bolt handles is an abomination for saddle scabbard use, although relatively few whitetail hunters use horses.

Some of the modern bolt gun's other highly touted attributes are of minor importance to the deer hunter. Accuracy? This is one of the bolt gun's claims to fame; but good non-bolt repeaters today can produce approximately two-inch groups at 100 yards, which is plenty good enough for even long-range deer work. Strength? The strong breeching of good bolt guns makes it difficult to blow one apart with an overload; but how many blown-up rifle actions of *any* kind have you ever known of firsthand, except when some shabby handloading was involved? Case extraction? The bolt gun's camming action makes for positive extraction, but only when the particular bolt model has a good extractor. The Remington 721–722 budget-priced bolt guns made after World War II were cursed with dinky extractors that could slip over rims and leave cases stuck in the chamber. Stuck cases hardly ever occur with modern ammunition from reputable manufacturers. And no handloader worth his salt should have the problem in the hunting field.

But even after those balloons are punctured by the needle of practical realism, the bolt-action rifle still holds that key ace of being able to handle the fairly long, high-intensity cartridges needed for long-range deer shooting. Most lever guns and lever-gun calibers don't have what it takes for this work. Except for the ancient Model 95 Winchester, which was made long ago in .30–06, the only other lever-gun cartridge that is genuinely efficient for consistent long-range deer performance would be the .284 Winchester, once available in the good Model 99 Savage. The .308 Winchester is chambered in Browning and Savage lever guns and might qualify as a long-range deer load, depending upon how much of an optimist you are.

The buyer of a bolt-action rifle in a big-game caliber in this country has, in the late 1970s, more than 50 rifles, both domestic and foreign, to choose from. Anything goes, from the little Savage .30–30 (no long-range rig, to be sure) on up to costly, handcrafted magnums with French walnut and gold-inlaid engraving.

That's too many models to cover in any detail, except in a book devoted purely to rifles. Even then, some of the material would be obsolete between the writing and publishing, since the market constantly changes. Foreign-import bolt guns and some semi-custom domestic makes by small manufacturers appear and disappear in a matter of months.

MODERN BOLT ACTIONS

To highlight some of the key models, modern bolt actions can first be divided into two classes: ex-military rifles converted to sporters and still found (sometimes as military issue) in every second-hand rack, and civilian-origin rifles.

Among the old military rifles, the most prominent is the beloved Springfield 1903 and its adulterated World War II version, the '03–A3. Often considered weaker than a good Model 98 Mauser, the Springfield still makes a fine sporter for non-magnum-length cartridges.

The redoubtable Mauser 98 design in general is with us yet, either as liberated military hardware, sold as issue rifles from various Latin American armories since World War II, or as civilian-made imported rifles or actions. Decent Mausers make excellent sporters once an inexpensive custom trigger unit is installed. Earlier Mausers of the so-called 93 pattern cock on closing rather than on opening, are thus somewhat slower in rapid fire, and usually lack a third locking lug for safety.

The term "Enfield" has confused many hunters. The 1917 Enfield was produced in this country from an original British design. It's a big, heavy action that, unlike the Springfield, can be modified to handle long rounds such as the .300 H&H Magnum. The other Enfield includes the various models of the elderly British service rifle, the so-called Lee-Enfield. It's a fast-handling rifle for a bolt action, but doesn't lend itself to classic sporter conversion and cannot handle high-intensity cartridges for big game at long range.

The fact that a few million Americans got bolt-action rifles in their hands during World War I led the American sporting-arms industry to seriously introduce bolt guns. Without delving into a lot of gun history here, the most important outgrowth of this was the introduction of the fabulous Model 70 Winchester in the late 1930s.

The Model 70 was considered the ne plus ultra of American big-game rifles until 1963. Beginning in 1964, Winchester adulterated the original design over cries of outrage by gun nuts. That's why you'll pay a premium secondhand price for "pre-1964 Mod. 70" when you find one—which is not always easy.

Between the World Wars, Remington played around with civilian variants of the heavy, unlovely 1917 Enfield. After 1945, the company boldly struck out into new design with the Rem. 721 and 722. These used some stamped parts that gun buffs never forgave, even though both actions were light, strong, economical to manufacture and buy, and had excellent triggers. Sensing that the consumer would pay more for a classier rifle, Remington abandoned the 721–722 series for a great design, the Model 700 series.

Remington was fortunate, also, in Winchester's unwise decision to go the opposite route in marketing strategy by cheapening the Model 70. Result: The Remington 700 rightfully inherited the de facto title of king of the bolt guns, although fans of the Ruger 77 and costlier Browning and Weatherby rifles might argue that.

For the whitetail hunter interested in a rifle with long-range capabilities, an individually good version of any of the bolt guns listed above (except the British Lee-Enfield) has possibilities. The Springfield and Mauser 98 admittedly are confined to cartridges of .30–06 length. However, a good '06 with appropriate loads makes a worthwhile long-range deer rifle, and can always be re-barreled to such formidable '06 derivatives as the .270 Winchester and the undersung but excellent .280 Remington. The latter rounds tread right on the heels of the popular (and ballistically overrated) 7 mm. Remington Magnum. The .300 Winchester Magnum is another fine cartridge for this work. So are the similar .300 Weatherby and .308 Norma Magnum, although the choice of rifle models is limited in these rounds. Going up in actual caliber, cartridges such as the .338 Winchester, .340 Weatherby and the Remington 8 mm. Magnum are usually too destructive on deer-sized animals. I base that on the amount of hash my .340 Weatherby has made on much bigger elk at 300 to 400 yards.

The best range of choices for the long-range whitetail rifle would be from the .270 to the big .30 magnums, with the .257 Weatherby as an exception, albeit a costly one. The 6 mm. or .243 Remington and Winchester rounds, the .257 and the .250–3000 all lack long-range killing power. So does the popular .25–06. My longest deer kill was at 413 paces with a .25–06, using a hotly loaded 117-grain spitzer, the best weight choice (along with 120-grain spitzers) for long-range work with the .25–06. The bullet luckily took the buck in the nape of the neck as he was going away from me up a steep hillside. Death was instantaneous, but even this hot load barely expanded and did not exit the relatively small mass of the deer's neck at this distance. Based on that mediocre performance by a maximum .25–06 load at what was probably a true 360 to 375 yards, I rate the .25–06 as not much more than a 300-yard deer cartridge. Incidentally, that .25–06 I used had a 26-inch barrel providing more velocity than typical sporters with 22- to 24-inch tubes.

For best performance, a long-range deer rifle requires experimental shooting with different brands of ammunition, bullet weights or various handload combinations to determine the ideal fodder. Don't automatically go for the lightest bullet weights and their high muzzle velocity. Medium-weight spitzers may have the longer tale to tell out at 300 to 400 yards.

The long-range deer rifle must be carefully sighted in. As a general rule for a high-velocity cartridge, 250 to 275 yards is the best compromise range for bullet strike to coincide dead-on with point of aim. Mid-range trajectory won't be high enough to cause a miss at intermediate ranges; and bullet drop at 300 to 400 yards, although a matter of several inches (depending on cartridge and bullet), will be manageable in terms of slight holdover on a deer-sized target.

One rifle-tuning feature I've found essential is to free-float the barrel on a bolt-action rifle used for hunting. That is, the fore end's barrel groove must be carefully enlarged, so that the barrel, except for a short length ahead of the action, doesn't touch wood. This frees the barrel from the accuracy-spoiling vagaries of the fore end swelling or shrinking slightly with humidity changes. While not a problem in arid country, this can be a real hassle when hunting in rain or wet snow.

Some fore-end bedding pressure on the barrel often makes a rifle shoot tighter groups. Usually this gain is not great in terms of big-game accuracy, and it's a total non sequitur if all-day rain causes stock warpage that puts Ol' Betsy's actual point of impact off several inches at long range.

That is a highly controversial point among gun nuts and gunsmiths. I'm only sharing a lesson learned the hard way in more than 35 years of big game and varmint shooting in various non-desert climates. Incidentally, unless you're skilled at stockmaking, have a good gunsmith with stocking experience do that barrel-groove relief job. It's trickier than it appears.

The bolt action is not the sole rifle choice for long-range whitetail work. You can get an accurate single-shot such as the Ruger or Browning in high-intensity calibers. The Browning BAR autoloader, mentioned in the brush guns chapter, has the necessary accuracy and is available in such rounds.

Long-range work is perhaps the only place where the modern single-shot rifles have any practical value as whitetail guns. Neither single shots nor bolt-action rifles are speed demons for repeat fire. This is no great handicap when hunting whitetails at long ranges along the edges of clearcuts or burns, however. A deer at 300 to 400 yards usually offers just one shot, and that's all. If you miss, that smoked-up whitetail is going to be in instant high gear for the nearest cover. Short of using a machinegun on a tripod, your chances of hitting him on a broken field run at almost a quarter mile can be considered nil.

A moral argument can be made that *running* shots close to timber cover should never be attempted at long range. One exception would be when the animal is already wounded, making it ethically imperative to try to anchor him at all costs. (I also yield that distant, running shots are more justifiable on mule deer or pronghorn in open country, where a wounded animal cannot easily escape. But such situations don't apply to whitetail hunting, since a whitetail will never be found very far from some good escape cover.)

THE DUAL-PURPOSE RIFLE

Is there such a thing as a rifle/cartridge choice that can serve both as a practical brush gun and still cut the mustard on any shots beyond 300 yards . . . in other words, an all-around rifle?

Yes, if you understand that such a compromise cannot be truly ideal for either of the two jobs. Looking for such a one-gun armory, I'd start with the premise that the typical whitetail hunter needs good brush gun qualities far more often than he needs good long-range rifle capabilities. The logical approach, therefore, is to pick a good brush rifle that also has both the cartridge performance and accuracy to put you in business with a buck on a distant hillside.

A Remington 760 pump in .270, .30–06 or (third choice) .308 is one example. It's an accurate rifle and poses less of a handloading problem than its companion 740 autoloader. In the latter, I'd opt for the .280 Remington as first cartridge choice. The Browning BAR in .270, .30–06 or .308 is a costlier choice than the 740 by more than $100, but is a surprisingly accurate autoloader. The BAR is also made in a magnum version for the 7 mm. Remington Magnum or .300 Winchester. The magnum BAR doesn't have the reputation for accuracy or reliability held by the model chambered for the non-belted '06-style cases. Mine in .300 Winchester is very accurate, however. A factory repair tune-up cured a serious jamming problem it had developed.

The point is, these potent pump/autoloaders are effective brush guns (though the BAR magnum version is a heavy rascal), and they can still do a number at long range. By contrast, bolt guns in equivalent calibers, while perhaps offering a bit more accuracy of

An example of a dual-purpose whitetail rifle suitable for close-range timber work and occasional longer shots, is this Model 99 Savage in .284 caliber.

A Remington 760 pump in .30-06 or .270 is a good choice for a dual-purpose deer rifle for either timber hunting or longer shots. This one has been modified with a custom buttstock and carries a Redfield 2-7X variable scope.

Bolt-action deer guns need not be heavy rascals. Ken Warner of the National Rifle Association publications staff packs this barrel-shortened Remington 600 in .308. With a scope and mount, it weighs just a few ounces over seven pounds.

For possible long-range shooting (despite falling snow), this deer hunter has a custom .300 Winchester Magnum with a 6X scope. Such a rig would be a poor bet in actual timber hunting, because of the rifle's weight, the narrow field of the 6X scope, and the unhandiness of bolt-actions in brush.

minor importance for big-game targets, would remain dismal brush guns for reasons cited in the previous chapter.

But never get carried away by ballistics sugar plums to the extent that you forget the importance of real marksmanship. A long-range rifle is useless without a skilled shooter.

5

Scopes, Sights and Mounts

For years, open iron sights were standard on American hunting rifles. Some of the fancier jobs were the "full buckhorn" type with curved-up ears around the notch. These made it easier to inadvertently shoot high, because of failure to get the front sight bead all the way down in the rear sight notch.

The best open sights were and still are fairly flat-top jobs with a shallow notch and no ears sticking up to obstruct your view of the game.

FRONT AND APERTURE SIGHTS

Front sights are either posts or beads. Shape is not as important for deer hunting as color. A black front sight can be tough to see in the poor light of evergreen timber late on an overcast November day. A brass insert in the sight is better, if you occasionally clean tarnish off to make it brighter. One that should be avoided in the north is a white bead front sight. It shows up well in poor light, but can utterly vanish from view against a background of hoar-frosted brush or snow.

Aperture sights—"peep" sights—are better than open sights for fast shooting, assuming you have a wide enough aperture to quickly see through. To prove this, a gunsmith buddy, Ed Ollila, once spent time getting very good with a receiver-mounted aperture sight, hitting targets thrown in the air. At his rural place of business, where it was safe to shoot that way, Ed loved nothing more than to get some self-styled expert to declare that, "Peep sights ain't fast enough for deer hunting." After the bet was made, they'd step out in back and Ed would proceed to pop small cans thrown into the air. This proved two things: (1) aperture sights are very fast on a moving target; and (2) only suckers bet on the other guy's game.

Don't depend on a new rifle to be sighted in. Take it where you can shoot from some kind of rest—a rolled-up jacket on the ground, at least—at a fair-sized paper target, and see where the bullets hit. At this point, even fairly experienced shooters get confused. You move the rear sight in the same direction you want your bullets to go. If the rifle shoots low, raise the rear sight. If she shoots left, move the rear sight right. It's exactly opposite with the front sight. Sometimes you move a rear sight as far to one side as possible, and the rifle still isn't sighted in. Then it's time to go to work on the front sight, drifting it in its dovetail with light hammer taps and a brass key to prevent marring the steel. But go opposite—to make the rifle shoot right, for instance, move the front sight left. Of course, you can't raise or lower front hunting sights except by putting in a higher sight or filing one down.

WHY A SCOPE?

Scopes on the market before World War II tended to be either very costly German imports or some pretty junky American-made jobs. Even the latter represented a sharp gain over the best of iron sights. A scope has several advantages. First, it gives a good, unobstructed look at the target and everything around it. Second, as long as you can see through it, you can't foul up your accuracy by sight misalignment because there's only one sighting element—the scope's reticule. Aligning that with the target must still be done correctly, of course, but you're spared the old deer hunter's bugaboo about those too-high shots because of a front sight not being aligned down into the rear sight's notch.

Third, a scope is a blessing for middle-aged farsightedness that makes it impossible to draw a good bead with iron sights. Fourth, the light magnification and simple alignment process of the scope makes accurate shooting possible in light that would severely hamper iron sight use. This is assumed to be dim light. Not always, however. Carrying an iron-sighted rifle, I topped over a low ridge overlooking a big alder swamp on a bright November morning. A buck and doe bounded in the alders and stopped. When I threw up my rifle, the glare of sun on the sights and particularly the fierce twinkle of sunlight on the heavily hoar-frosted alders made the deer vanish. Lowering the gun, I could see them again, but not over the sights. Eventually they took off without a shot being fired. If I'd had a scope, that buck's liver would have had an evening dinner date with onions.

There's a sequel, and it ties in with the first and most important lesson on scope use in timber. Back at the cabin for a mid-morning coffee break, I disgustedly hung up the iron-sighted rifle and grabbed a Mauser .257 with a 4X scope. An hour later, making a drive for others, I jumped a nice buck out of a swale only 20 feet away. Two big leaps carried him into a clump of young balsams, where he spun around to see what I'd do next. That's rare cooperation from a whitetail.

Looking through the scope, all I could see was an over-magnified, out-of-focus maze of evergreen twiggery. The crosshairs of this scope, an early Weaver K-4, were also too fine for this work and tended to blur out of focus at the present range of maybe 20 yards. I simply could not find the damned deer! In the few seconds that I frantically fished around with my eye and scope, he spun and took off.

Within the space of a couple hours, I had had two good buck chances ruined by opposite extremes of sighting problems—first not having a scope, and then having too much scope.

The moral of the second problem is that low-powered scopes with fairly heavy reticles are best for hunting timber, where game shots can be awfully close. Here, you don't need the superior accuracy that a scope's naturally finer alignment provides. What you want is the speed of aiming and clear-look field of a scope. But higher-powered scopes, as cited, can ruin you in close-range timber.

The scope's field of view is important. This is rated at the number of feet wide the field of view is at 100 yards. Typical 4X scopes such as the old Weaver that I used that morning have about 30 feet at 100 yards. That meant only a six-foot field at the 20-yard range where I was trying to pick up that standing buck. A low-powered scope of 2 to 2½X would have been good for an eight-foot field, which just might have helped, particularly since the close-range images also would have been substantially sharper at a lower magnification.

There are a number of good, fixed power scopes of 2½X magnification on the market. If you hunt fairly close-range forest and brushlands all the time, stick one of these on your rifle.

But here's the Catch 22. If you hunt where long shots are available—the kind of setups described in Chapter 4—more magnification can be vital in a scope. Hunting western whitetails along a wooded creekbottom, I cut over a ridge to pick up the next segment of bottomland. Four deer along the timber edge at about 275 to 300 yards were grabbing a last mouthful of alfalfa before drifting into the cottonwoods to bed down for the day. My eye caught a gleam of sunlight on an antler. Through the 2½X scope I was using, I couldn't pick out which deer wore horns, since they were backgrounded by a lot of antler-resembling dead cottonwood branches. Needless to say, I didn't get a buck that day.

That was in the days before good, variable-power scopes were on the market. At first, variables were bum-rapped as being nonsense. Friend, I remember when they said the same thing about hydraulic brakes and automatic transmissions! Granted, some of the early variables were both optical and mechanical dogs—not very sharp images and prone to mortal sins like shifting zero when you changed power. But most variables today are good, and some are excellent—for a higher price, understand.

VARIABLE SCOPES

Variables fall into three general power ranges: 1½ to 5X, 2 to 7X and 3 to 9X. The 1½-5X variables are the most useful. At their low setting, they provide huge fields of view—60 to 70 feet, or much more than the good 2½X fixed-power scopes. Their higher magnifications are suitable for deer shooting at long range.

The 2-7X models typically have low-end fields of 40 feet or better, approximating the 2½X fixed powers. Their higher power is most useful for sizing up a buck's rack at a long distance or doing some distant ridge scanning in lieu of binoculars.

The 3-9X models are a bit too much for a whitetail rifle. Their low range usually is about 35 feet, less than optimum for close-range timber hunting. Their very high magnification on the other end is much more than a big-game hunter needs. They're costlier than lower-range variables, tend to have less optical sharpness and more internal flare problems, and are heavier. They're bigger scopes with more impact-vulnerable overhang, and their larger objective (front) lenses require undesirably high mounting.

The latest trend in scopes is toward wide-angle models with rectangular ocular lenses. These definitely add more field of view at any power. For example, the Redfield 3-9X in the wide-field version has almost 40 feet of field at 3X. But the problem of size and weight remains. Stick with a smaller range variable, and you'll be happier.

FOGGING, OTHER PROBLEMS

Although optics, mechanical ruggedness and accuracy of elevation and windage adjustments are a light-year ahead of scopes made only a generation ago, some manufacturers still have problems in moisture-proofing. Internal fogging is the big-game hunter's worst scope problem, except for some unlikely impact bad enough to knock a scope out of zero.

Unfortunately, advertising claims don't always match performance in moisture-proofing. Most scopes today are filled with inert nitrogen and then sealed. If the seals leak, the nitrogen is replaced by air, and condensation can take place with temperature changes. In three seasons running, I had three different Redfield scopes fog on me, which might be a record. None were dunked; they just fogged up in cool, wet weather typical of fall hunting. I brought this to the maker's attention and, since then, Redfield has changed its sealing system. To give the company credit, my factory-overhauled foggers haven't done it since. In the Northwest, where I live now, veteran hunters swear by the Leupold scopes. These are made in Portland, Oregon, where presumably the designers know what cool, wet hunting weather is.

Generally speaking, you get what you pay for in scopes. Low-priced scopes are more prone to problems than the topline makes such as Leupold or Redfield. I had a fairly new Weaver variable simply shed its ocular lens as I slipped the gun out of a case. A friend of mine had a Tasco variable's insides fall apart. A Montana chum, who used to do a lot of guiding, said he saw so many customers' cheaper scopes fail that he started bringing along a loaner rifle in a scabbard on a packhorse. The only makes he hadn't seen go bad were Bausch & Lomb (now off the market), Leupold, and Redfield.

Scope problems convinced me to use an easily detachable mount, which allows me to switch to auxiliary iron sights. When my last Redfield fogging failure occurred, I was two miles from camp in good deer country. The late-afternoon witching hour was approaching. Fortunately, the unusable scope was in a Weaver flip-over mount that allowed use of iron sights. I also use the better (and costlier) Pachmayr swing-over mounts, which allow total removal of a scope, yet retain zero when remounted. Neither make has given me any trouble, and they've held zero during scabbard transportation on trail bike, horseback, 4WD vehicle and light, vibration-prone aircraft.

Another system is a high-mounted scope with a tunnel mount that allows use of open iron sights. This is a fish-nor-fowl deal, however, that puts the scope too high for quick aiming.

That golden oldie, the Winchester lever-action 94 and its variants, can't use a conventional, center-mounted scope (explained in Chapter 3). Two solutions exist, however. One is an offset mount that puts the scope tube clear of the 94's cartridge ejection path. The other is a long eye-relief scope mounted on the barrel. This looks weird but works fairly well. Don't be spooked by the narrow field of view ratings for such scopes. When you mount it that far forward, you can see around the scope at the same time you're seeing through it.

Whatever kind of mount you choose, screw it on for dear life. Wash out screw holes and screws with alcohol, dry them, and then use a thread sealant such as Loc-Tite while sinking the screws with a screwdriver that fits well without slipping to mar the slots. Hex-headed screws are offered by some mount makers and are better. Make sure the scope is not mounted too far to the rear, where it could give you a nasty cut on the eyebrow from recoil in a shot uphill.

Reticles available in American scopes today range from the classic crosshairs to dots, posts, tapered crosshairs and duplex (thick and thin) crosshairs. For forest hunting, crosshairs are okay if not

The Model 99 Savage has been a deer-hunting favorite in various forms for three-quarters of a century. This one has iron sights that become usable when the scope is tipped to the side. Such a dual-sight arrangement is a blessing when conditions prevent use of a scope.

Hunting from a tree stand and elsewhere in timber requires a bold, clearly visible scope reticule.

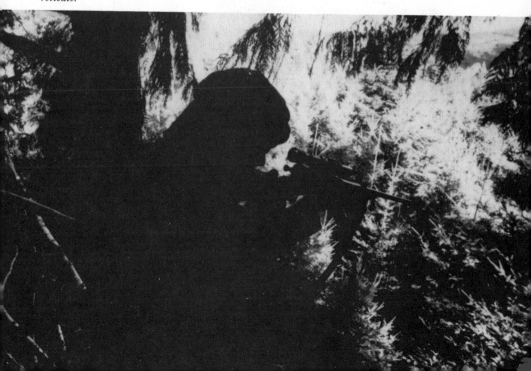

too fine. A post reticle or thick-bodied duplex crosshairs is much better. Forget dots; at close range, they're much too small to pick up against dark timber backgrounds unless mounted on clearly visible crosshairs. I tried to defeat that problem by getting T. K. Lee, inventor of the modern dot reticle process, to make an oversize six-minute dot for me. It subtended six inches at 100 yards, but was still too small for fast aiming at 25 to 50 yards in dark puckerbush.

Various gimmicks to cover scope lenses against rain and snow are on the market. The only ones worth considering are those that come off instantly with a flick of the finger, either from mechanical springing or an elastic loop. Properly installed, these work and are a good idea for anyone who hunts in rain and particularly in snow.

A high-quality, well-mounted scope is a very durable instrument. But in summary, I again recommend a quick detachable or flip-over mount with auxiliary iron sights—just in case. All told, I've had five scopes fog on me, and two went out of action in the field due to mechanical problems. In most cases, I kept on hunting, thanks to quick-detachable mounts or flip-overs and iron sights. Once, however, I stood for an hour on a deer stand, waiting for some hard-working drivers to come through, while I held a scoped rifle (without iron sights) fogged so badly that I couldn't have seen the lights of Broadway through it. If a deer had come out, I'd have shot from the hip, I guess.

That tore it. Despite scoffs by the experts over the years about back-up iron sights being unnecessary, every deer rifle I own now wears scopes *and* iron sights. Amen.

6

Smoothbores, Blackpowder and Handguns

SLUG SHOTGUNS ON DEER

For many American deer hunters, the question of the right gun is very simple: They must use shotguns, either by law or because of geophysical factors.

The shotgun hunter is not ill-armed if he picks a 16- or 12-gauge firearm. He has the option of several models of fast-handling weapons, some specifically tailored for deer use. A shotgun is also one way for the beginner on a tight budget to arm up for deer. A decent 12-gauge bolt-action shotgun today runs over $100, and a trifle more for a special deer model with sling and swivels. A single-shot is considerably cheaper. They aren't Brownings or Weatherbys, but they will take deer.

I've only been at the post-mortem of two shotgunned deer. One of these was hit at a long 100 yards by a school teacher buddy who didn't realize that distance was too far to try with a shotgun using only the front bead. He blithely shot at the head for a quick kill. The slug, as luck would have it, entered one ear and exited the other. The brain-shot deer died before its knees even buckled. But that placement proves nothing about slug killing power, since a .22 LR bullet would have been fatal in the same place. Some days, a greenhorn just can't do anything wrong.

The other incident involved my son Peter's first deer. The 14-year-old kid had showed some wingshooting ability with his featherweight Model 12 Winchester shotgun, but so far hadn't calmed down enough to do well in rifle practice. I decided to let him use the shotgun, because at least he had confidence in the smoothbore. A Williams receiver sight was installed and the weapon sighted in for 50 yards with slugs. I stuck Peter on a good deer stand and worked a drive to him. The unmistakable boom of a shotgun echoed.

Yes, a deer had come by, and Peter had fired. And missed, he said with all the wide-eyed tragedy that implied for a youngster who'd been looking forward for years to his first deer season.

But the tracks on the deer runway showed enough brownish-gray hair to stuff a small pillow. Careful trailing eventually revealed blood and finally a dead deer almost 125 yards away. It had taken a perfectly placed hit in the ribs right behind the near shoulder. The trotting deer's shoulder was swung forward, or the slug would have hit shoulder bone. At a 25-foot range, the slug had flattened like a watch fob under the hide on the far side—and I mean flattened. On recovery, it resembled a battered silver dollar.

But despite getting clouted by more than 1500 foot-pounds of slug energy, that relatively small doe (legal in our zone that season) had showed no immediate sign of a hit. She certainly wasn't clubbed off her feet, as many hunters expect of a close-range shotgun slug.

Peter's experience remarkably matches that of a large number of shotgun slug hunters censused during a deer hunt on the 16,000-acre Crab Orchard National Wildlife Refuge in southern Illinois. In the 1970 issue of *Gun Digest*, a yearly publication worth any gun hunter's attention, author Art Reid reported the Crab Orchard findings.

According to Reid, some 582 deer were taken with slugs in the first three days of a 10-day special hunt (to thin an overpopulated herd). Almost to an animal, the deer had to be blood-trailed, often as far as 100 yards. Most deer didn't show clear signs of being hit. Reid and his hunting partner riddled Reid's buck, a 180-pounder, with five 12- and 20-gauge slugs before it went down 52 yards away. Another hunter hit a spike buck (weight not given but probably not large) three times in the chest cavity with 16-gauge slugs, but the buck made it 70 yards before it cashed in.

This and similar studies tell that slug guns will kill deer, all right, but rarely as quickly as higher velocity rifle bullets of similar energy. Energy is achieved two ways. One is weight of the missile; the other is speed. Of the two factors, I'd rate speed as having more lethal effect, given reasonable bottom limits of missile weight. A 12-gauge slug has plenty of weight (typically one ounce or 437.5 grains, which may vary from slug to slug). But it has only about 1400 foot-seconds of muzzle velocity, and its shape slows it down much faster than a typical rifle bullet. Although a 12-gauge slug has an adequate 1500 or so foot-pounds of energy at 50 yards, it loses a third of this at the 100-yard mark.

For perspective, the impartial and certainly well-qualified Sporting Arms and Ammunition Manufacturers Institute does not recommend ammunition for deer that develops less than 975 foot-pounds at 100 yards. The .410 shotgun slug, with less than 300 foot-pounds at 50 yards, is hopeless. The 20-gauge slug, weighing only 275 grains, has a marginal 900-plus foot-pounds of energy at 50 yards and a dismal 630 foot-pounds at 100 yards. If the 20-gauge slug is a decent deer load, then so is the .30 carbine, a cartridge damned by all authorities for deer hunting even when expanding bullets are used. It practically equals 20-gauge slug energy performance out to 100 yards.

Frankly, I'd rate the 20-gauge as a doubtful deer gun. Sure, it will do the business, when everything goes right. If anything goes wrong, such as a shot being less than perfectly placed, then there's just too much chance of a wounded and lost deer. I do not believe that any hunter, whether out of ignorance or as a form of warped ego trip, has the right to hunt game with inadequate weapons.

There are three drawbacks about shotgun slug shooting. First, the guns are not quick deer killers, as we've seen. Second, the typical shotgun lacks a good sighting system, unless one is installed or unless the gun is made specifically for deer hunting (as some makers do). The usual, unsighted shotguns are not easy to shoot accurately. That's unfortunate, because if anything the shotgun slug needs more careful placement than the typical deer rifle bullet to get quick, knockdown kills.

Finally, the shotgun slug combo is used in a lot of mid-continental whitetail areas where rifles are ruled out for farm safety reasons. That's fair enough; but such geographical areas usually lack snow in deer season, making it more difficult to track wounded deer.

Don't take all this as damnation of the 16- and 12-gauge slug guns, even if the 20 slug is of dubious value. A 12- or 16-bore, with a decent rear sight that's sighted in to put the slugs where they belong, will kill deer well. Slug guns are capable of three- to four-inch groups at 50 yards. Imported European slug loads in some cases do better (but are amazingly expensive).

Since shotgun slugs don't take deer as quickly and violently as higher-velocity big-game rifle loads, the burden is on the slug gunner to shoot carefully, to never take doubtful shots, and to do a conscientious job of tracking any shot-at game. The stubby shotgun slug is a relatively poor penetrator, and should never be used for rear, going-away shots on deer.

Just remember that the slug gun, even with good sights or a scope, is no more than a 75-yard deer weapon in terms of consistent performance. Steel yourself to resist the temptations of longer shots commonly available in more open farm country, where slug guns are often the only legal weapons and where crop-fed deer are often pretty big animals.

BUCKSHOT ON DEER

The use of size 0 or 00 (called double-ought) buckshot for deer is largely limited to the South. Northerners often sniff at southern use of buckshot and hounds in hunting. But if you've ever seen or tried to penetrate the incredible density of Dixie canebrakes and pocosins, you'll understand that hounds for moving deer and buckshot for shooting deer are the only practical systems in much of the South.

Basically, buckshot loads have even less effective range on deer than slugs. Experts point out that the thin patterning of the shot even on deer-sized areas, coupled with the relatively dismal ballistical qualities of round shot, make buckshot loads a poor bet beyond 40 yards or so.

Shotguns are notorious for being finicky about buckshot in any size. The only thing to do is actually pattern an individual gun. Sometimes a double gun will pattern one size of buckshot nicely in one barrel, while the other barrel does best with a different size. That's good to know before a big buck comes by, outrunning the hounds.

Even close in, the relatively small missiles as a rule don't clobber deer off their feet. The most articulate buckshot hunter was Archibald Rutledge, a southern gentleman who killed more than 300 bucks in his life with smoothbores, in a state (South Carolina) with multiple bag limits on deer. If you read Brother Rutledge's excellent writings, you'll

58

note that a great many of those deer traveled a way before folding up. With good hounds, quickly finding those dead deer was no problem, even in the near-jungles of lowland South Carolina. But a hunter using buckshot without dogs may have a tracking problem, especially since buckshot wounds are small and don't permit much blood sign.

Buckshot never has been popular with northern hunters, even where permissible. In Washington State, for example, where buckshot is legal and the forests can be mighty thick, I've never known a deer hunter who used it. Old-timers in the Midwest and Northwest tell me that buckshot's last stand among northern hunters was during the Depression years, when many a rural family had to take deer, legally or otherwise, to augment their meager rations. Such families often couldn't beg, borrow or afford a rifle. Even then, I am told, a preferred practice was to open the mouth of a paper shell and drip in enough candle wax to hopefully bind the buckshot into a solid mass. Assuming this crude form of old-fashioned artillery case shot didn't come unglued on firing, it broke up on impact and made lethal, multiple-wound channels. This way, at least, all the shot charge hit the deer instead of half or more of the pellets tangenting off to miss. *Don't try it, however, because the addition of the wax weight to the shot charge is almost certain to run up firing pressures that can endanger both the gun and the shooter.*

For buckshot use in dense southern forests, I'd get a good, open-choked smoothbore and test it to see how well it patterns different brands of 00 buckshot shells. The use of granular plastic buffering and shot wrappers has improved heavy shot performance, with fewer deformed shot flying off cattywampus. Since decent buckshot patterning is something of a lottery at best, I'd use 12-gauge 2¾-inch short magnum loads holding more shot. Even better would be a three-inch magnum 12 such as the Remington 870, which puts out 15 double-ought buck, compared to nine in the conventional 12-gauge 1¼-ounce load and 12 in the 1½-ounce short magnum.

Not to be overlooked among deer-hunting smoothbores are shotgun-rifle combinations. These have long been favorites among Germanic hunters after a variety of game on one hunt, ranging from hare to hirsch (a large deer).

Such firearms hold some interesting possibilities. Obviously, a hunter carrying a charge of buckshot and a deer-sized rifle cartridge for instant, optional use has something of the best of two worlds, closer or farther out. A similar program is used by some southern hunters. In eastern North Carolina, for example, a favorite system is for Zeb to take a stand, armed with a rifle *and* a buckshot-loaded smoothbore, while Zeke gets a mile over on the next rural road and turns the dogs loose. The rifle is handy across portions of clearcuts or agricultural fields. If the deer breaks cover close by, the shotgun comes into use. Both alternatives in one gun would be one solution to this problem.

Combination rifle/shotguns are also being sold to hunters in states offering fall turkey seasons that overlap deer seasons. Here, the hunter can pack a load of heavy bird shot, such as No. 2, for any gobbler opportunities and still have a rifle shot instantly available for deer. That's not too shabby an idea for a deer hunter in good grouse country, substituting lighter shot for the smaller birds. Even western chukar partridge and deer opportunities can similarly overlap, although deer jumped on chukar hills are likelier to be mulies rather than whitetails.

BLACKPOWDER WEAPONS

Much of what has been said about the tactical use of shotguns on deer applies to blackpowder muzzleloaders. Most of the charcoal burners don't compare in power to smokeless powder big-game loads and should not be used for dicey shots or longer ranges.

The booming (no pun intended) popularity of muzzleloaders has led to a rash of state legislation. Many states allow special "primitive weapon" hunts for true muzzleloaders. But check your state regulations. Some impose minimum caliber sizes and barrel lengths. Unless quite recently changed, Pennsylvania law allows only flintlocks. Wisconsin allows just smoothbore blackpowder arms for hunting, unless that too has been changed.

One rule in picking a blackpowder rifle is to get a hefty caliber. Beginners might think a .40-caliber muzzleloader is a small cannon. But a .40-caliber round ball weighs only 96 grains and would be driven at too modest a blackpowder velocity to provide much energy. To get equal .30–30 Winchester performance at 100 yards calls for a quite large, .58 muzzleloader, a conical bullet instead of a ball, and from 120 to 140 grains of FFg (granulation size rating) blackpowder. Since conical bullets like the well-known Minie ball (the great killer of the Civil War) have much longer effective range than round balls, they may be ruled illegal for safety reasons in certain areas. Minies and their modern-design counterparts are no slouches as missiles. One Minie-cast design

60

Blackpowder rifles like this percussion-lock Enfield musketoon replica have become increasingly popular for deer hunting in many states.

in .45 caliber will weigh close to 290 grains, almost the heft of a .58 round ball.

Serious blackpowder hunters (which I am not) tell me that the great problem today is one that originally afflicted archery hunting. Smitten with the lure of extra seasons or special hunts in areas closed to smokeless powder weapons, too many hunters just dash off to buy the first muzzleloaders they see. Blackpowder weapons take some special understanding to get good results, and should be used only within their ballistical limitations.

HANDGUN HUNTING

Even more demanding than the blackpowder gun in terms of required expertise and conservative application of hunting ethics in deer hunting is a handgun. Used by an expert pistol shot, a high-intensity handgun such as the .41 Magnum or .44 Magnum is a fairly formidable deer killer up to 100 yards. (They'll kill beyond that range, but getting well-placed hits is the hooker, even with a scoped handgun.) The problem arises when some dude buys himself a big handgun, which is hard to shoot accurately without lots of serious practice, and sallies forth to make like Marshal Dillon against a difficult game target like the whitetail.

Anyone who aspires to hunt deer with a handgun owes it to the game to first make himself not just a good but a superb pistol shot. That is not easy; it requires lots of time and ammunition. After becoming expert on the target range, he should do some serious handgun hunting on small game.

Even so, the handgun in deer hunting should be limited to fairly close range shots where the shooter is reasonably sure of a vital hit in the chest cavity or the sure knockdown of a shoulder hit. Head or neck shots are condemned by good handgun hunters as too chancy except at very close range. Probably the most legitimate use of the handgun is in close-range trail-watching, which offers the best chance of a quick-killing shot on undisturbed, slow-moving deer.

I regard handgun use as legitimate only in a limited range of whitetail hunting situations, and then only among a relatively small number of expert gunners who can accurately kill deer and not leave lost cripples as raven bait. Because of those narrow and specific limitations, I can't give handgun models, calibers, loads and shooting techniques enough priority to warrant the two or three full chapters that proper treatment would require.

Many books exist on handgun hunting. But a lot of hard, consistent practice on the range and in small game and varmint hunting must be done before the handgun hunter should try for deer. Just don't tell 'em that ol' Nels here sent you. Even though I was a pistolero addicted years ago to shooting easily dispatched snowshoe hares on the run with a .22 Hi-Standard HDM target handgun, I'm not keen about big-game handgun hunting except when done by highly qualified experts.

7

"Sure As Shooting" Marksmanship

Marksmanship for the hunter of whitetail deer involves two problems. One is hitting the game on the run at closer ranges—where it will often be running because of the hunter's proximity—and the other is shooting at slowly moving or standing deer in the distance. As we saw in Chapter 4, the sportsman has no business trying to hit whitetails on the run at long range.

Flat-trajectory modern rifles and greatly improved scope sights seem to hold out promise of making long-range shooting easy. Don't kid yourself. A deer at 300 yards or more is a very small target for any gun. They're not really easy to hit beyond, say, 100 yards, in the opinion of many hunters.

MASTERING THE BASICS

The whitetail hunter whose country offers some long-range prospects must master basic marksmanship, starting with the fundamentals of trigger squeeze and breath control.

Begin by brushing up on basics in the marksmanship manuals from the National Rifle Association, the various gun and ammo makers or any of the many good shooting books on the market. If

Good hunting marksmanship starts with enough target practice to master the fundamentals of sight picture and trigger squeeze.

When a formal shooting range isn't available, a hunting rifle can be sighted-in where safe, legal shooting conditions permit. The varmint scope on this pickup truck's hood serves as a spotting scope to observe bullet placement on a 100-yard target.

access to a big-bore shooting site is a problem, a great deal can be learned from practice with a good .22 rifle or even an indoor air rifle. These should have scope sights that somewhat match the scopes on big-game rifles. Even the experienced marksman can keep his hand and eye in trim for the real thing by practicing with a small-bore or air rifle.

With fundamentals mastered, the deer hunter striving to become a good long-range shooter can do no better than to get in some varmint or small-game hunting that puts a premium on rifle accuracy. Woodchucks, rockchucks, crows, prairie dogs, ground squirrels, foxes and coyotes can all provide demanding sport. The late Jack O'Connor, Mr. Rifleman to millions of American hunters for decades, said that what skill he had with a rifle was largely acquired and polished by shooting desert jackrabbits. Hunting squirrels with a scoped .22 in lieu of a shotgun is fine training for the big-game hunter.

WHY HANDLOADING PAYS OFF

Your marksmanship will be polished brightly by practicing with your actual hunting rifle. This can be expensive. Some types of big-game cartridges are retailing for 60¢ and more a round in the standard boxes of 20; and certain magnum loads can cost you 75¢ or more per bang. Unless you're well off, much shooting at those prices will blow a major hole in your wallet. Handloading, however, brings the cost down about 60 to 80 percent, depending on whether you're reloading new cartridges or your own salvaged empties. Gun clubs often have access to shooting components at wholesale prices for their members. Casting your own bullets for reduced-load target shooting is even cheaper. At 10 to 12¢ a round, a hunter can afford a good deal of target practice without taking out a credit union loan.

Some shooters hold off on handloading because they think it's a difficult or dangerous art, requiring profound knowledge beforehand to stay out of trouble. It's not difficult, it is safe, and it doesn't require great expertise—just common sense at following rules.

At least two dozen reloading books are on the market. That lodestone of all shooting expertise, the National Rifle Association, 1600 Rhode Island Avenue NW, Washington D.C. 20036, puts out a fine manual, *The NRA Handloaders Guide.* The frequently updated Speer Bullet manuals are very good. Along with similar manuals by other bullet makers (Hornady, Sierra and Nosler), these list proper bullet/powder combinations in various calibers. These recipes are usually conservative enough to prevent potentially dangerous over-charges. But starting from scratch with any rifle, it's always wise to begin two or three grains (of weight) under the recommended charges and work up from there. If you begin to have extraction troubles or excessively flattened primers on the empties, your loads are too hot for your rifle and should be reduced.

Be meticulous in your handloading. Sloppiness can cause trouble. Never mix powders. Be sure each cartridge has a powder charge in it before you seat the bullet. A primer alone has the power to lodge a bullet in the barrel. And then, when the next fully charged round is fired, it can blow up the barrel, the action, or the shooter a bit in the process.

Bolt-action rifles are best for handloading. Other types of actions should not be ignored, however. Pump and lever actions can be handloaded successfully. The trickiest to handload are cartridges for autoloading rifles. By their nature, they're more finicky about their fodder.

We Americans have a tradition of firearms marksmanship. But you can't inherit such skill from your ancestors or a history book. Read about rifle marksmanship. Study the fundamentals. Then go and do it . . . lots of shooting between seasons and particularly just before season.

HITTING GAME ON THE RUN

Hitting a moving target with a single bullet is an art. No memorized mathematical formula can solve the problem when a buck suddenly tears out of his hidden bed and starts bounding the windfalls. There are too many variables, from his speed to your reaction time. At such a moment, instinct based on previous moving target shooting is the only alternative to blind luck. But familiarity with your rifle, scope, and trigger squeeze will help.

Even with the fairly high velocity of a modern rifle bullet, you have to lead or shoot in front of the point where you hope to hit that deer. The surest shots I've known were all experienced shotgunners

on upland birds or waterfowl. If you're not a bird hunter, a fair amount of skeet shooting will give your eye/hand reflexes valuable experience in that necessary split-second computation on how much to shoot ahead of a moving target.

As many or more deer are missed by shooting over them as by under-leading them. In too-hasty shooting with a shoulder weapon, there's a strong tendency to not get your head down on the stock. Holding the head too high causes you to shoot high—exactly as if you had a rear sight set much too high.

With open iron sights on a deer rifle, the same problem exists. The buck comes into sight, the shooter throws up his rifle, aims with his front sight—and shoots too high, because he didn't have his head down and failed to notice that his front bead was not down in the notch of his rear sight.

Scopes and aperture sights (the kind with a hole in them mounted on the extreme rear of the rifle action) aren't as bad. You can have your head a bit high and still get a "truthful" picture of scope crosshairs and target. Aperture (or "peep") sights for big-game hunting have a fairly sizable hole. The eye tends to center itself in the middle of that aperture, because that's where the maximum of light is coming through. If your head is too high on the stock, you can't even see the front sight through the receiver sight's aperture. Presumably, you'd hunch your head down to see the front sight before trying the shot, unless you're so rattled that you fire an essentially unaimed shot.

Although the scope makes it hard to overshoot because of too-hasty cheeking of the rifle, you can still overshoot a deer with ease. A bounding whitetail is a high-speed optical illusion. Although he doesn't have the high, pogo-stick gait of a fleeing mule deer, the whitetail's long bounds are still taking him a few feet into the air. He may also make some deliberately high leaps to clear some obstacles. Your eye and brain are fooled into thinking he's well up in the air all the time, because he shows up most prominently at the apex of each of those bounds.

I greatly prefer to plan the shot where his leap is bringing him down, while at the same time picking a hole in the brush through which I can fire. Tough and complicated as all this sounds, it's easier than some types of bird shooting, such as picking off ruffed grouse in timber. Remember that in many of these running white-

69

The elusive quarry may not offer a second chance, so quick, sure marksmanship is required of the whitetail-deer hunter.

tail shots, the game is likely to be pretty close—20 to 40 yards. Sometimes closer!

Out of fairness, I should add this. Some good deer shots I've known try to pick off the bounding buck in the air rather than at his lowest point as he hits the ground. My father, who's been hunting deer since before the Kaiser's War, is fond of this in-the-air shot and rarely misses.

How much lead is required? At these typically close ranges, the crosshairs are just barely ahead of the deer's brisket or front chest line as my gun goes off. Like most moving-target shooters, I can't give any better description than that. Bear in mind that deer have different gaits, ranging from walk to trot to all-out bounding run, and require different leads for different speeds.

If the deer at close range is going away at about a 45 degree angle, I still have some space showing between the sight and his shoulder, with the intention of angling a bullet in behind his near shoulder.

But these are only rough guidelines, because each shooter does it his own way. A gunner taking a very fast, swinging lead, as if he were making a broad streak with a paintbrush, may think he's not leading at all but firing right at a running deer at full deflection, or 90 degrees. However, even if the shooter is fast, there's still a slight lag in trigger pull and lock time for the firing pin to fall and the rifle to discharge. By the time those things take place, the muzzle has swung ahead of the running deer without the shooter realizing it. He remembers his brain willing the shot when the sights were right on the deer, but the shot was fired with the barrel ahead of the deer, even if only a little bit.

Here's one of the most important tips in bagging deer on the run: Sometimes, a sharp whistle or shout will stop a fleeing whitetail in his tracks. It works best if a deer driven or jumped by someone else comes tearing past you. The whistle or shout will often cause the deer to slam on the brakes and try to locate this new menace. If you're quick-witted enough to remember this trick, it can mean the difference between a chancy shot on the run or one at a standing deer. But don't expect it to work on a whitetail who's on the run from you and who already has a pretty good idea where you are.

The easiest running deer to hit is the one coming straight at you or going straight away. Some hunters argue that a rear-end shot is never justified. At longer ranges or with cartridges of modest power

70

or bullets of poor penetrating qualities (for example, shotgun slugs), this is true. But it has exceptions. I've shot several deer that way and never lost one. Typical modern deer cartridges have plenty of power at timber-hunting ranges to drive a well-expanded bullet up into the target's engine room from behind. The raking shot can cause more tissue damage and hit more vital organs (spinal cord, liver, heart, lungs, diaphragm, aorta) than the shorter, trans-chest path of the classic broadside shot.

The problem of the rear-end shot is that it's messy to clean the deer afterwards. The broadside chest shot is cleaner in this respect. But the broadside hit is not always as instantly lethal as the hot-stove pundits like to think. A deer shot through the lungs or heart often manages a wild, 100-yard dash before going down. Much of the typical bullet's energy is wasted as the missile passes through airy, unresisting lung tissue and exits beyond.

DO'S AND DON'TS

There are some common-sense restrictions. A rear-end shot, like those from any angle, is never justified on a poorly aimed, desperation basis. It should be taken only when the shooter is reasonably sure of a square and fair hit that kills or at least quickly anchors the game.

Second, the shooter should always be prepared for a fast follow-up shot to prevent a wounded animal from escaping. Third, rear-end shots shouldn't be attempted with low-powered, marginal rifles or with stubby, high-speed bullets that may not penetrate all the way through into the lung/heart area.

True, a poorly placed rear-end shot will hit a hindquarter and ruin a lot of meat. That can also be done at a quartering angle or even in a badly aimed broadside shot. In one of my less inspired moments, I jerked off a badly aimed shot at a broadside buck at about 60 yards that ruined *both* rear quarters, impossible to do with one bullet in a rear-raking shot.

Another area of controversy in deer shooting is the neck vs. chest hit. When I'm sure of the shot, I'll try for a broadside neck shot. Head on, the neck is a slender target except at the closest ranges; and the hunter then might be wiser to aim for the broader target of the frontal chest.

71

Deer's neck is a smaller target than the chest and shoulder area. But on this buck, the neck offers a clearer shot than the chest.

The danger with hasty neck shots is not just a clean miss, but a non-anchoring hit in the animal's jaw. That probably won't bring him down, and a second shot may not be possible.

As a rule, try for a forward chest hit on a deer. That may mean damaging some eating meat on a front shoulder or both of them. A shoulder hit, however, kills more quickly than a hit in the chest ribs alone.

All this sounds clinically grim. If the act of killing bothers you, don't hunt. Otherwise, do your very best to make quick, humane kills. This calls for developing both your own shooting skill and your judgment about when a shot should be taken or passed up. Along with safe shooting habits and the Golden Rule application of the sportsman's ethic, those are your fundamental responsibilities in deer hunting. If you can't cope with the whole package, you don't belong in the hunting field.

8

Extra Equipment Makes Life Easier

In addition to his hunting togs and firearm, the deer hunter should have other items as well; some he will need, and some he will want for convenience' sake.

KNIVES

Some hunters sally out with knives that are much too large. A four-inch blade is plenty of knife, not just for deer but for bigger game too. One of my favorite deer-cleaning knives is a jackknife with a slender blade, which is ideal for a clean, rear-reaming job.

Two basic types of big-game hunting-knife shapes exist. One has a dropped blade. That is, the upper line or false edge of the blade droops down in front, putting the actual point close to the longitudinal center line. This makes a narrow tip, needed for neat incision work on a game carcass. The other, less pointed style sees the back line of the knife blade continuing straight, with the cutting edge below sweeping up to make the point. This results in a more sharply rounded cutting arc, the most useful blade for skinning. Some knife makers compromise between the two shapes and create a knife that's useful for both incision work and skinning.

74

A knife made specifically for skinning is usually kept in camp, as a deer carcass is rarely peeled in the field. The knife taken into the field for incision work should be as good as you can afford, since cheap hunting knives don't hold an edge and can break unexpectedly.

In picking a knife, pay attention to the sheath. Good knives come with good sheaths. A bad sheath can lose your knife afield or cause you serious injury from your own blade. Never carry a fixed blade knife in a sheath on your body unless it's safely around the corner of your hip, over one buttock or the other. A knife on the side is uncomfortable against your pelvis, can make a noisy clink against your rifle, and is easily pulled out of its sheath by dense brush. A knife carried on the front of your belt is extremely dangerous. In a bad fall, it could penetrate the sheath and plunge into your upper thigh.

These potential dangers are why some hunters prefer a folding knife, either for sheath carrying on the belt or in a pocket (less secure against loss). Make sure a folding knife has an open blade lock for safety in use.

Knife sharpening bedevils many hunters. The best way to sharpen a knife is to use a substantial Arkansas oilstone and make slicing strokes as if you were whittling the stone. The stone should be oiled first. With practice, you'll learn to keep an even or consistent angle on the bevel you're grinding into the blade, with a curving slice to sharpen the upsweep to the tip. Final stropping on leather or cardstock will help hone the edge. Don't try for a finely angled bevel that's sharp enough to shave hairs . . . that's too fragile for the rough work of cutting belly rib cartilage on a deer.

Don't abuse a good blade, regardless of the quality of steel or maker's claims. Some hunters hammer knives like chisels to split the pelvic cross-members of deer carcasses. Unless field quartering is essential, I skip that step in order to save my blade's edge. The pelvic job can be done with a hatchet or axe back in camp. Never use a good knife for throwing practice, and don't use it for opening tin cans except in real emergency.

ROPE AND DRAGS

Whitetail carcasses are usually taken out of the woods in one piece. Except on a horse hunt, this means dragging the carcass.

Carrying one over the shoulders is impractical with big whitetails and too dangerous in most areas. Tying a whitetail to a pole for tandem carrying by two people is miserable—the carcass swings and bounces, painfully hammering that pole into the shoulder. Gimmicks such as one-wheeled stretchers to take out a deer are nice, but only if terrain permits. All too often it does not.

In the big-turnout whitetail states, opening weekend usually sees newspaper headlines such as "Four Dead as Deer Season Opens." Often, you'll find that half or more of those hunting fatalities are not because of gunshot mishaps but, rather, heart attacks. Of these, I'll bet 90 percent occur when a middle-aged, overweight, out-of-condition hunter is trying to drag a deer. The moral: Don't kill yourself in this task. Take it easy, get help, or quarter the deer and take it out on the installment plan.

For dragging a deer alone, use thick rope that won't cut deeply into your shoulder. Trice up the head and forelegs, and keep the drag rope short enough to help lift the feet and nose slightly clear of the ground. Years ago, I had a factory-made towing harness of simple nylon straps, like suspenders, with a hook where they joined between the shoulder blades. This was far better than the usual over-shoulder rope drag and left both hands free for carrying the rifle and pushing brush out of the way. That harness got lost somewhere, and I keep vowing to make a new one, since the design was simple. It featured a horizontal strap across the chest, so my whole torso was used in the drag.

A good solo drag trick, if you have enough line, is to tie the ends of the line to the opposite ends of a stout stick about 30 inches long. Then lay out the line to form a vee. Use that centered vee of line to trice up the deer's head and feet. Then step inside that vee, get your chest or pelvis up against the horizontal drag stick, and start moving. Since you may need both hands to help regulate the stick against your body, this works best when you have a sling on your rifle to free both hands for the dragging job.

Two hunters can drag best if the towline is tied to a stick long enough for both of them to hold about chest high and then lean into it in parallel. They can each have a hand free for their guns. A stick drag or the use of a nylon body harness is fine with one-quarter-inch nylon line that otherwise does a painful shoulder-cutting job.

More hunters should consider quartering a whitetail if facing a

Dragging a big buck, even on snowless ground, is relatively easy for two hunters using a crossbar long enough for them to throw their bodies against it across the pelvic or chest areas. Note that their arms, which tire quickly, need to be used only to help hold the bar in place.

bad drag. Years ago, one of our party of four knocked over a big buck far back in a villainous country of northern Minnesota hogbacks. The kill took place around 1:00 p.m. We dragged that buck until dark, three guys pulling and one carrying four rifles. We left the deer, hiked out to the road in the dark, came back at daybreak, and worked until noon to bring the prize to the road. That was about 32 man-hours of murderously hard work, even with snow to ease the drag friction. Quartered, that deer would have packed out in one trip on four backs that same afternoon. Having packboards or big Poirer-style packsacks—either back at camp or in the car—makes sense when hunting bad terrain.

In a really remote hunt, you can always quarter and then bone out a deer, eliminating packing out the substantial weight of the skeleton. Know in advance if your state game regulations require packing the head along for legal proof of sex; most of them do.

GENERAL GEAR AND GADGETS

Compasses will be covered in detail in Chapter 14 on Woodcraft. Consider a good compass to be as essential as your hunting britches. I know a few hunters who consider compasses to be sissy stuff. I also know that these characters have wasted more time lost than they care to admit, and often come out of the timber in much different places than they intended.

If you hunt alone, a very lightweight rope hoist is useful to get a big deer hung at the kill site for skinning and quartering. Otherwise, there's no need for a hoist when hunting, useful as they are back at camp.

If hunt movies or snapshots turn you on, packing a camera is feasible in most whitetail hunting situations. Movie cameras have gotten larger and heavier in recent times, thanks to features like battery-driven motors and zoom lenses. If you want some good Super-8 shots of the boys coming through on drive, better figure on a daypack to carry your camera with you.

Conversely, still cameras have gotten smaller. The little miniatures of the Kodak Pocket Instamatic type are truly shirt-pocket size and produce good snapshots or passable slides. Capable of better photo quality are pocket 35-mm. cameras, which are not much bigger than a pack of king-size cigarettes. Three I can recommend from experience are the Minolta Hi-Matic F, the Olympus 35-RC and the pocket Rollei 35.

A deer hunter with long-range shooting aspirations sometimes has a problem knowing the range involved. Distances can be deceptive. Rangefinders small enough to pack along on a day's hunt are available. Not that you're likely to have time to fiddle with one when a whitetail is sneaking along the far side of a clearcut or opposite ridge. Rather, the logical use for a pocket rangefinder is to first take a reading on an area that you plan to cover. The Rangematic model is usefully accurate when directions are followed. It's given me some surprises and saved me some useless shots. On one occasion, I took a reading on a clearcut's far side. What I had eyeballed as about 300 yards or a bit more was very close to 500. A dip in the lay of the land made that far side look much closer than it was. The Rangematic is a bit too big for actual pocket use, but can be carried in a belt sheath (provided) or, better, in a daypack or game pocket.

PACKS FOR DEER HUNTERS

For years I hunted without a daypack. After I started using one, I couldn't understand how I had gotten along without it. A small pack is dandy for packing lunch, survival gear in country where it may be needed, a small flashlight for an unexpected late trip out (ever try to clean a twilight-shot deer after dark?), a topographic map of the area, a rain garment, and a canteen of water.

Two kinds of daypacks are available. One conventionally rides on your shoulders. Don't pick the cheapest model, and pay attention to the quality and width of the shoulder straps. The second type is a fanny-pack that straps about the waist and rides on your hips and upper buttocks very comfortably. For ducking under lots of brush, the fanny-pack is quieter.

Unfortunately, no outdoor manufacturer to my knowledge has put a woolen daypack on the market. I have one, custom-made, and it's far quieter in the woods than the noisy texture of the typical nylon pack.

This fanny pack (made by Aspak in Colorado) is a durable job that rides comfortably on the hips and doesn't get caught on brush as the hunter crouches.

Many whitetail hunters don't carry binoculars, but a pair can be useful even in many forest situations.

BINOCULARS

The whitetail hunter can rarely use a spotting scope except in some specialized cross-canyon setups. Binoculars are handy if they're: (1) broadfield enough to be useful in timber; and (2) light and compact. With a pair of Bushnell Custom Compacts in the 6X25 size, from a tree stand I spotted a whitetail sneaking through brush that I could hear but could not spot with my eye or my $2\frac{1}{2}$X scope. These binoculars provide a field of view of about 42 feet at 100 yards, which makes them practical for timber hunting, and the 11-ounce weight is light enough. Another alternative is an ever-smaller, lighter monocular.

WALKIE-TALKIES

Unless your state game laws forbid them, walkie-talkie radios can be useful in some deer hunts. Twenty years ago, I experimented with small, $\frac{1}{10}$-watt walkie-talkies on the CB wavelength. These were marginally useful in flat, heavily timbered country but could be counted on up to three quarters of a mile. Much better are more powerful (and heavier) 5-watt WT's. Intermediate sizes in 2- or 3-watt range are almost as heavy and expensive as 5-watters, so you might as well choose the latter size. You will need a free Federal Communications Commission license, using an application form available from any Citizens Band radio dealer.

Our hunting crews have never used two-way radio in hot pursuit of game and have never expected to. Rather, the use has been in calling the crew together for getting out a deer or in keeping track of each other's whereabouts, which has obvious safety value. When the youngest hunting crew member, then aged 12, knocked over his first buck, he was able to call in a couple of us oldsters to field-dress it for him by way of instruction.

The best way to use walkie-talkies in a hunting group is to establish a predetermined "network check-in" time—say, every hour on the hour. That prevents unnecessary monitoring and chattering between times. In situations where even low talking into the radio might screw up the hunting, a predetermined signal system can be used by simply pushing the transmit button without speaking. The other set will hear the transmitting set's carrier wave (sans voice) click on—for example, two clicks can mean: "I'm in my original location and am staying here," or whatever you arranged.

But check out the legality of walkie-talkies in your state's hunting regulations booklet, and familiarize yourself with the federal regulations. And don't clutter up the channels with that pointless good buddy jazz just to play with the radios.

BAGS AND CUSHIONS

Most deer are shot by hunters who are stationary for some reason. Successful stump-sitting starts with being comfortable enough to stay still for long periods. A plastic bag makes a useful waterproof seat on a snowy log, stump or rock, and can double to carry out heart and liver. An inflatable rubber camp pillow is my favorite to keep my aging haunches warm, dry and comfortable. Also available are safety-colored vinyl cushions for this purpose, but they're bulky enough to require a daypack to haul them any distance into the woods. If all this sounds effete, so be it. I've never seen where avoidable discomfort either got me more deer or was good for my soul.

AUTOMOTIVE AIDS

Short of trying to steal someone's deer, breaking game laws, or hiring a camp cook out of a massage parlor, your likeliest unscheduled trouble in deer hunting is automotive. Except for rural residents who hunt their own lands, most of us use motor vehicles to take us where we're going to hunt.

This is not a section on automotive care and repair, but a quick primer on vehicle and driving aids useful for the hunter, particularly when he gets off the main highways. A few weeks before writing these lines, I was towing my 16-foot travel trailer through a snowstorm at night on a hunting trip. A trailer tire blew. Problem: no spare, which is stupid. Okay, pull the wheel and drive into town for a new tire (if obtainable at 10:30 p.m.). Problem: new, never-used hydraulic jack doesn't work. Unwise of me never to have checked it out before this. Problem: In the darkness and snowstorm, other traffic endangered me at work on the narrow road shoulder. I had flares in my pickup truck and couldn't find them. Not very smart and could have gotten me killed.

Here's a list of items that may keep you out of vehicular trouble or help solve problems that do arise.

Carry a good tow chain, steel cable or nylon towing strap. Except in very large sizes, sisal and polypropylene ropes are undependable. A slight towing assist from another vehicle may save a lot of jacking and digging or make it possible to bring your broken-down vehicle to a repair place.

A good jack is priceless. Unfortunately, the jacks that come with new vehicles are often junk and can even be dangerous to use. A strong bumper jack is still the best rig for quickly raising a vehicle's corner off the ground for tire-changing or getting unstuck. Hydraulic and scissor-type axle jacks are more stable to use, but they don't have great height of lift and may require two-step jacking and blocking.

For backroad use, a basic set of pioneering tools includes a good shovel or spade and an axe. Along with a workable jack, those items can do wonders to get you unstuck. Automotive repair tools should include two good screwdrivers (slot and Phillips head), a pair of vise-grip pliers that make a good emergency wrench, and perhaps an inexpensive set of socket wrenches. A full roll of plastic electrical tape is handy for wiring repairs (a problem area with trailers) or for a short-term patch job of a ruptured radiator hose.

Make sure your spare tire is sound, and ascertain that Teenage Son hasn't absconded with the lug wrench from your vehicle. Using aerosol-can tire-inflators, I've yet to reinflate a flat tire enough to risk even short-range, low-speed driving. But such cans do contain a sealant that's usually capable of stopping off the puncture leak (big tire breaks or blowouts obviously aren't helped). After that, the punctured tire can be reinflated with a hand pump (hard work) or from a portable sportsman's compressor run off your 12-volt system (Coleman Inflate-All or other makes—$40 to $50).

Three decades of winter driving in northern states convince me that snow tires do provide extra traction in loose or wet snow. They aren't as good as conventional treads on packed snow, ice or wet pavement. When conditions are bad, old-fashioned chains work wonders, nuisance though they are. Carry some stout baling wire and a few mending links for any chain repairs.

Buy a five-foot hunk of standard (non-industrial) woven-link (cy-

A flashlight carried in a daypack can be your best friend in helping you clean a late-afternoon deer kill or find your way back to camp after dark.

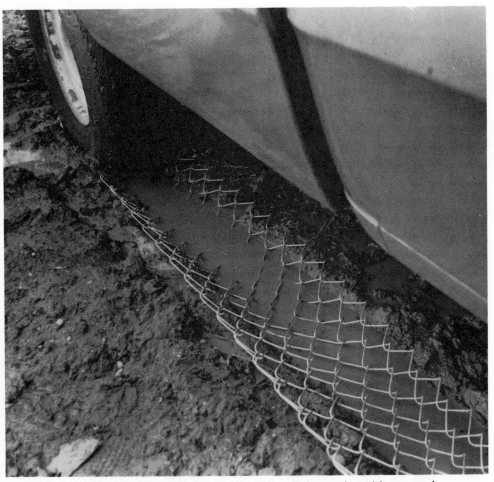

Just two small sections of woven-link fencing take up little room in a pickup or auto's trunk, yet they provide traction when the going is sticky. For deep snow, nothing beats tire chains.

clone) fencing in the six-foot height. The dealer will show you how to easily split that five-foot span into two 2½X6-foot pieces. These make quick-lay treadways under your driving wheels in sticky going; and the two treadways take up little flat room in a vehicle trunk or truck box. They're lifesavers at times.

A hunter with a two-wheel-drive vehicle can risk questionable back roads if he has a winching system. Three main types are available. An electric winch (several on the market) for about $400 has enormous pulling capacity to get you unstuck. Power winch systems for about $125 fit on most chain-saw models and produce enough geared-down power to pull out a badly mired vehicle. Finally, a ratchet winch of the old come-along style (beefed-up version of a farmer's fence-stretcher) will work wonders, albeit very slowly, for about $50.

In any back-country trip, I carry spare motor oil. A chum of mine once knocked out his oil-pan plug on a back road. He could whittle a stick to hammer-plug the hole, but meanwhile he'd lost his oil and couldn't run the engine.

In warm country, an extra jerry can of water is always good. If you break down in the boondocks, you won't go thirsty. Or if you blow a radiator hose and get it taped up, you'll still need refill water for the radiator. In cool, wet or cold country, a can of anti-icing compound in the gas tank prevents fuel-line freeze-up. No hunting vehicle is complete without a first-aid kit, a spare key cached securely somewhere, flares, and a good flashlight.

A few elements of a car or truck are both likeliest to cause a breakdown and can be checked in advance. Before the big trip, start your engine and put a hand on the alternator housing. If a bearing is going bad (common failing of alternators), you'll feel the vibration. Check the drive shaft universal joint, particularly if rough driving in steep country is ahead of you. Examine the fan belt, and look for any leakage that may be starting around the water pump. Best, of course, is to have a trustworthy mechanic check your rig before a major hunting trip.

Finally, have a radio for weather reports. News of a coming bad storm may save you from serious trouble.

9

Secrets of Learning Where and How to Hunt

The best deer hunters I've known have been a very mixed jar of pickles. Some were hyper-energetic, some were lazy. Some were superb marksmen; others were indifferent shots. Some were old, some were young.

But they all had one trait in common. Each of them knew his hunting area in detail—the lay of the land, the way deer used that area, and dozens of physical features.

Here's an example of how important this can be. For decades, my father and Uncle Ralph hunted near the family cabin in northern Minnesota. In fresh tracking snow, Ralph jumped a buck, too close to dark to do much about it. That night, as an all-ears 13-year-old (campbound, alas, by a touch of flu), I heard them lay plans. The known factor was that the buck was in a dense black-spruce swamp forest several acres in size.

"He'll leave that swamp tonight to feed on higher ground, but he'll be back into it before daylight," Ralph declared. "I won't see him when I jump him tomorrow in that thick spruce, but with the new snow, I can stay on his track until I run him out of there."

"Where will he go out?" my father asked.

Ralph glared at both of us for emphasis and stabbed the map with his finger. "If the wind holds northwest, that's where he'll come out, right at Martin's Narrows. He'll be going like hell up-wind across that open strip to reach the timber ridges on the other side. That isn't his real destination. You see, Mr. Buck in this cold weather wants a nice, windproof, black spruce swamp for bedding. When I finally annoy him right outta this one, he'll run into the wind, into those ridges north of the Second Lake, to reach those other spruce swamps up there.

"Now, it's going to take me two hours to haze him out of the swamp he'll be in at daybreak. You've got a long wait covering the Narrows, and you'd better be there when he comes out."

So it happened. Dad trekked into the narrow opening of the abandoned homestead between the swamp and the higher, timbered ridges. He'd just finished checking his watch—one hour and 55 minutes—when he heard Ralph's faint, upwind hail, "He's commmming!" A minute or so later, dad heard the rhythmic "huff-huff-huff" of a hard-running deer. A fine eight-point whitetail buck in all his glory came bounding out of the black spruce and sprinted with that racehorse gait of a worried whitetail crossing open ground. The buck's nose and shoulders plowed a neat furrow of snow for several yards after a single shot broke his neck.

That was a simple but classic example of knowing the area and how deer use it. Seemingly, there were a number of places that buck could have gone when tired of Ralph dogging his backtrail. As anticipated, the buck killed almost two hours by first trying to shake Ralph. Their trails zig-zagged and figure-eighted many times.

Finally, the buck decided there'd be no rest for him here this day. Most of the adjoining area was also timber. But Ralph's logic was correct. The buck wanted other spruce swamp cover, he preferred to go upwind to reach that, and this route took him across the narrows.

Ralph never saw the antlered quarry until he came up to the kill scene. "I knew he was going to beeline out the narrows when his trail quit turning and made a straight line toward the northwest edge of the swamp," Ralph explained. "That's when I hollered that he was on his way out."

Dad and Ralph knew that country from many seasons of hunting it. The learning process is speeded by pre-season scouting, which saves precious hunting days from being wasted on tactical errors through inadequate knowledge of the terrain and deer usage.

KNOW YOUR QUARRY

A deer's lifestyle is fairly simple. First, he needs a food and water supply. Second, he always needs cover for concealment and at times for protection against inclement weather.

Deer are lazy. If a deer finds a place where his bedroom and dining room are in the same place, great. Usually, the two are in separate places. But for whitetails, these will be fairly close together.

Most good whitetail deer country has physical variety. Perhaps the ideal situation consists of fat farms broken up with plenty of dense, brushy forest. Deer will raid crops at night and use the adjacent timberland for daytime bedding. Start by finding deer trails from forests to fields. Usually, deer will pick the shortest route that offers good cover and the chance to travel into the prevailing wind.

If your hunting country lacks croplands, look for old forest-fire sites (harder to find these days, fortunately) or recently logged areas. If there's some standing water nearby (marsh, stream or lake), there'll be whitetails around.

Locating such areas cold-turkey can be done several ways. One is simply to take the motor-touring time to scout around. Your state game department personnel can be of help. If your state has a well-run deer-management program, department personnel should have detailed deer-kill records by areas. These will help you start looking.

Other good information sources are foresters, loggers, rural mail carriers, school-bus drivers and highway department workers—people whose jobs take them back and forth in the countryside. A farmer or rancher, of course, knows pretty well what the deer situation is on his place but may not know much about other areas.

A bartender friend of mine drives to his rural home from work after closing at 1 a.m. He's thus on the road during the witching hour when big bucks are feeding and on the move. Several times one fall, he saw one big buck crossing the road. Scouting out the place in daytime, he found a well-packed trail, lots of big, dew-clawed tracks and the large droppings typical of big deer. With a companion, the thoughtful mixologist moved in on opening day, worked a couple of simple drives, and nailed apparently that same big buck he'd often seen at night.

PRE-SEASON SCOUTING

Once you pick an area that supposedly has a good deer population, get out on the ground and learn it, finding out the key trails, browse or feeding areas, bedding areas, good deer stand sites and accessibility to get yourself into those places. Pre-season scouting is detective work. It takes a lot of time. You can't learn much about an area in an hour or two.

The road system needs study and correlation with whatever maps you have. Some newer roads may not show on older maps. Conversely, older backroads shown on maps may turn out to be no longer passable. In forested country, roads are built for logging. After a timber harvest, such roads may be abandoned for years, with bridges falling into decay, culverts washing out, and young trees, brush and blowdowns blocking the right-of-way. Forest roads that are okay in summer's dry weather may be impassable during fall rains. Conversely, some forest tracks that are too muddy in summer may be usable after freeze-up.

Make notes in your scouting work. Use a notebook or a tape recorder. A camera is useful for photographing the lay of land from a ridge, fire tower or light aircraft. Air reconnaissance reveals a lot of ground quickly; deer trails across marshes or other open ground can sometimes be seen easily from several hundred feet in the air.

U.S. Geographic Survey maps are accurate for showing land forms and basic cover types (green for brush or timber, white for cleared land), but may be years out of date for showing roads. Such maps also can't tell you important details. Let's say such a map shows a swamp. What kind of swamp? You have to find out firsthand. A cattail marsh may be an important deer hideout. A timbered swamp can be a favorite hidey-hole for whitetails. Lots of standing water may keep deer away unless they're hard pressed, although they may still use it if there are small, dry islands on which they can bed down. You have to study such things not only in terms of their usage (or non-usage) by deer, but in terms of their effect on your travel. Most swamps are difficult for a hunter to traverse quietly, and some can't be traversed at all.

Scout first to find feeding areas. At this point, you must know something about what deer eat in that region. Your game department probably has publications that provide this information. All deer like some farm or ranch crops. Alfalfa is a favorite. They'll

Here the author does some riverside pre-season scouting with a canoe. Deer tracks are visible in the soft shoreline.

Whitetails favor densely covered bedding areas that offer both concealment and protection against harsh weather.

Whitetails are fond of swampy cover like cattail marshes, unless icy conditions cause too much noise and potentially painful travel for them.

Section corners on U.S. Forest Service lands are usually marked with yellow metal "location posters." A nail driven into the appropriate corner of the 36-section grid shows hunter this exact location. Never damage or remove these markers. This is a good spot to double-check your location by using map and compass.

browse in timothy hay meadows at night in the fall, too. Corn, cabbage, garden produce and rutabagas are all eaten with relish by whitetails, as many an exasperated farmer knows. Apple orchards are magnets for deer.

A detailed list of natural whitetail foods is of no value here, because it can't be localized to your area. The bewilderingly long list of whitetail foods in the South's fecund climate means nothing to the whitetail hunter of the Lakes States or Rocky Mountain West. But, regardless of geographic region, the natural deer foods are low-growing shrubs and young tree growth still within reach—for example, black ash sprouts in the Lakes States. Some non-brush foods that deer universally go for include acorns and some other hardwood mast and wild mushrooms.

But since deer generally prefer low, brushy vegetation, it's best to scout such areas while looking for neatly clipped twigs, deer tracks and droppings. You must look carefully to see these things. Deer are epicures. They often do their woodland browsing by taking a nip here and a nip there, picking the more tender twiggery on a shrub and leaving much of the rest untouched.

To repeat, your local game department personnel can be invaluable sources of information here. You may need to learn some Boy Scout-level botany from available pamphlets or local library books, but that's not difficult. Knowing the key deer foods of your area and then knowing how to identify those species in the boondocks is extremely important and well worth mastering.

Deer diets often change with the season. Fireweed, a common plant in recent burns or logged areas, is a favorite late summer food of deer, but their usage of it drops off in the fall. Shallow-water aquatics are eaten by whitetails. But since such water plants often shrivel in the fall, deer quit feeding on them after summer. A marshy forest pond that you've seen deer feeding in during the summer may no longer attract them in, say, November.

Don't overlook water availability. Whitetails don't like to travel far for water.

After finding active feeding areas, your logic should tell you where to look for bedding areas. They'll tend to be up the prevailing wind from good feeding areas, they'll be on dry ground (perhaps even on islands or hummocks in wet, swampy ground), and they'll have good cover. That doesn't mean big timber. Mature forests often don't have much undergrowth, and it's the low growth that deer bed down in for both shelter and concealment.

They'll use different bedding areas in different weather. Cold, windy weather often drives them into tall grass or cattail swales if they can find a dry spot to curl up. Rain or snow pushes them into areas with low-spreading young evergreens. Very warm Indian summer weather makes whitetails, now wearing their winter coats, seek shady, cool spots, like northern ridge faces. Conversely, they'll prefer southern exposures to pick up any sun available on cold days.

Look for flattened, circular spots two to three feet in diameter in the grasses and ferns. Those are deer beds. They don't use the same beds night after night, but they may use the same area repeatedly in given weather circumstances.

There will be a variety of trails. The normally used trails will take easy routes between feeding and bedding areas. Deer often move in the dark and avoid trails in obstacle-ridden places for that reason. Easy, nighttime trails are often not used in broad daylight due to lack of concealment. On a timbered ridge in whitetail country, you'll typically find a well-used trail along the ridgetop's more open timber where the going is good. Drop down the ridge to thicker cover, and you'll find another parallel trail. The hunter should cover the latter trail, because the odds are strong that's the one deer would use in daytime.

There's another trail category of importance to hunters. Look for lightly used but still discernible deer runs that go from bedding areas through dense cover into even denser cover. These are escape routes. Does and fawns will sometimes use the more open trails to flee when spooked, but the bucks are much more likely to split along better concealed routes.

As you wander about in a whitetail neighborhood, take notes to help remember the trails. They're the key to most whitetail success. Pay attention to other things besides the telltale clues of where and how deer use the area. Look for good standing sites to cover such areas. If there's a considerable distance of a few hundred yards (which is considerable by short-ranging whitetail standards) between identified feeding areas and main bedding areas, you have a chance of intercepting deer moving just at dawn or before sundown. More likely with whitetails, however, is the chance of ambushing deer on escape routes from bedding areas. Big whitetail bucks are canny enough to be in their bedding hideaways before daybreak

Scouting for deer sign before season can reveal bedding areas used by whitetails. Notice the small area of depressed grass, where a whitetail has bedded in mild weather.

and often don't leave them to feed until after dark. With them, your best chance of an interception is on an escape trail when they've been kicked out of a bedding area by another hunter. One exception is during the rut, when bucks do some irrational things, but that's covered in Chapter 10.

FINDING A PLACE TO HUNT

Along with the matter of whitetail scouting goes the problem of the land being open to hunting. Depending on where you live, this can be the most crucial problem of all in this age of more hunters and more land closed to hunting.

First, a "no hunting" sign isn't a final block. Landowners usually don't want uncontrolled numbers of strangers hunting all over their land. Often, a landowner will permit hunting if the hunter appears courteous, safe, sane, and responsible. Some landowners actually want hunters. Orchardists, for example, can take a fearful beating from too many deer. Some landowners who practically hang out the "Hunters Wanted" sign are the commercial timber companies. Too many deer raise hob with reforestation, nipping tops off young seedlings. A vast total acreage of commercial forest land in the United States is owned by such companies in the West, South, Lake States and Northeast. Most of it is open to hunting, both to keep deer depredation within reasonable bounds and as a public relations gesture.

The things any landowner fears are unsafe practices (shooting around dwellings and livestock), careless damage to roads in wet weather, leaving gates open for livestock to stray, and sheer vandalism. The latter is a serious problem with forestry firms. There's definitely such a creature as the slob hunter, and he's the deadliest anti-hunting enemy that real sportsmen have today. These gun goon types ruin it for everyone. Many of them, admittedly, are not hunting as such when they shoot up highway signs, logging equipment, or occasional livestock. But sport hunters as a whole get the public blame for it.

Approach a private landowner well before season to get hunting permission. Be civil and straightforward. Don't con him that you plan to hunt alone when you actually plan to appear with half a dozen buddies on opening day. Honor any particular restrictions he has, such as not hunting a specific area with livestock in it. Don't get hostile over a refusal; it's his land. If he says no, inquire if he knows of other landowners who accept hunters. He may know several.

Actually, there may be more public land open for hunting in your area than you realize. Much of the land in the West is in National Forest or Bureau of Land Management status. There's also plenty of National Forest land in the Lakes States and the South. Various states have large acreages of state forestry land open to public hunting. Some federal wildlife refuges allow deer hunting to keep animals from getting too numerous. So do some state game refuges. Some state game departments over the years have acquired lots of land specifically for public hunting. Pennsylvania has more than 1 million acres of such lands, for example. These areas naturally draw lots of hunting pressure. Console yourself that many opening-weekend redcoats aren't very effective hunters, and that plenty of whitetails are still available later, when much of the crowd has quit and gone home.

Little known is the fact that many states, at the time they were formed, set aside lands in public trust, often for school-funding purposes. One common pattern was to reserve one section out of every 36-section township. Typically, these "school lands" are open to hunting, but check with your game department to make sure. The next problem is finding such sections. You'll need township section maps, available from the auditor's office of the county you plan to hunt, and a car with an accurate odometer to measure distance.

A section is one mile square. Public roads often run on section lines. After an initial orienting of where you're starting from, you should be able to find a public section by keeping track of distance on the road network. It becomes trickier on foot in an area lacking roads, of course, and you may need some sketch map help from the auditor's office or the nearest public forestry office.

Some states simply lack much public land. Texas, the best deer state in the Union, is the prime example. Most hunting in that state is done on private lands, usually for a fee. Another approach is to form or join a hunting club that leases land. Deer-hunting clubs are common in some Southern states and parts of the Northeast. Membership accessibility varies from one club to another. Pay-as-you-go hunting, once you line it up, solves a lot of problems. The landlord usually knows the best game areas, for one thing. Lack of hunter competition is a key advantage.

Whether for fee or gratis invitation, never forget that you're a guest when on private land. Conduct yourself as a sportsman. That doesn't mean you can be an irresponsible slob when on public land, either.

10

Buck Behavior in the Moon of Madness

Against one of the world's smartest game animals, the whitetail hunter needs all the help he can get. His best aid comes when the game makes mistakes that briefly tilt things in the hunter's favor. The most important of these mistakes are likely to be during the annual rutting madness of the whitetail buck.

One of the whitetail's characteristics is great sexual aggressiveness. The whitetail buck goes loco during the rut—unbelievably so at times. Northern Indians justifiably called the November period coinciding with the deer-rutting peak the Madness Moon. Most hunters believe the rut is brought on by cold weather. Although frosty nights may make the sex-fevered buck even more restless, reliable studies show that a change in the angle of the sun's rays as winter approaches is what brings does into heat. (Penned does can be brought into heat by changing the angle of artificial lighting.) The rut occurs earlier in the North and later in the South. In the tropics, the little Guatemalan whitetails mate year-round. With no winter, fawns can be born anytime.

One important factor for the deer hunter in the United States is that whitetail bucks start getting the urge before the does get the urge. I've seen rutting behavior in whitetail bucks in late September and early October in a northern state where does go into oestrus, or

The buck who left this rub mark on a white cedar will be at his most vulnerable when the mating season begins.

heat, well into November (which could be as late as January down in Arizona).

The whitetail buck getting ready for mating undergoes a ritual of making ground scrapes (typically a couple hundred yards apart) in his home territory. He'll paw the ground to bare earth and urinate in it to leave a scent calling card. Often, he'll attack a nearby shrub with his antlers in apparent mock combat. Plenty of ravaged shrubs in an area mean lots of buck activity. While I've never seen any proof that a buck regularly goes back to a sapling rub, I do know that they keep returning to their earth scrapes. The urine-scented scrape is his way of advertising that he's very definitely "at stud" to service any willing does. A doe in heat will often paw around such a scrape and urinate there herself, thus setting up a tryst that Big Daddy can easily track her to, once he finds her "advertising" at his scrape.

PICKING A STAND

Years of studying buck scrapes in my personal north-woods hunting area showed that most of them were on or close to major whitetail trails from feeding to bedding areas. Some scrapes were exposed in open timber, and others were down in swampy glens. But rarely were they very far from main deer runways. Obviously, a deer-hunting stand location covering a main trail between a couple of scrapes (preferably in good view of one scrape) is one of the best spots a deer hunter can find. All he needs then is patience. Very heavy hunting pressure can throw things awry, however, keeping uneasy bucks on the jump so often that they can't concentrate on running their "rut routes" until nighttime.

Sometimes it's better to pick a stand site covering the runway between two known scrapes, rather than to set up a stand directly covering one scrape. One year my Uncle Ralph dragged me off into the woods a weekend before the season to show me two big, fresh scrapes along a deer trail. Running between the scrapes, the trail cut through a white cedar glade. Ralph axed off some higher cedar limbs to build a ground-level blind covering the trail, meanwhile explaining his strategy. Why not an ambush directly covering one of the scrapes? "I don't know for sure which way Mr. Buck is going to approach those scrapes," Ralph answered. "It depends on the wind direction. As he gets close to a scrape, he may leave the trail to circle it first, testing for scent. If I'm there, he may smell me before I get a good shot at him."

Ralph continued that in his view the connecting trail was a better bet, since the deer would predictably be on it, one way or another. The stand was set up on that side of the trail least likely to be the wind direction. The cedar patch itself had some advantages, Ralph explained. First, the dense cedar canopy had little undergrowth beneath it. That, with the wet, mossy forest floor, would make it possible for the hunter to walk fairly quietly to the stand before daybreak.

Second, the strong aroma of the fresh-cut cedar boughs would help mask residual scent of the hunter on stand. Third, the cut cedar at that time of year was a food bait for any deer, including wandering does. If they started frequenting the area to nibble the cedar boughs, normally out of their reach above the "browse line," it made rutting buck traffic all the likelier on this trail.

Ralph's tactical insight paid off with a handsome six-pointer 15 minutes after the season began the following Saturday.

One of the stranger cases of getting a big whitetail buck easily due to the rut happened to my hunting partner Jim McFall, who left his car on a road and crashed carelessly into an alder swamp to start a drive toward me. Just then a big buck slowly got up out of a bed only a few yards ahead. He promptly went down with a 170-grain slug through the neck.

We were mystified. Normally, a big whitetail buck doesn't bed that close to a road once the deer season is on. Second, the noise of Jim stopping the car, slamming a door, and clumping into the alders would chase out any buck in its right mind. This mature buck had simply offered himself as a sacrifice as haplessly as if he'd walked into the cabin at lunchtime to surrender.

The mystery cleared up when we skinned him. The buck's entire rear was a mass of small-diameter bruises, although his thick winter coat had concealed the damage until skinning. The small size and multiplicity of the bruises ruled out injury from auto impact, which would have left one or two massive larrups. Obviously, the wounding agent had been another buck's antler tines.

As we reconstructed it, this buck lost a duel the night before in the large, deer-rich forest across the road. Snow tracks showed that he'd come across the road, entered this alder swamp, and then bedded down for some hours, judging from snowmelt in the bed. In that time, he apparently stiffened up so badly from the gouging that he just couldn't get up and move until it was too late. Jim said that the dreamlike slowness with which the buck stood up in front of him was the damnedest deer behavior he'd ever seen. Normally, a buck that close to getting stepped on would take off as if rocket-assisted.

Though whitetail buck battles sometimes end in death for one contender, or both if they lock antlers and starve, the typical engagement ends in one buck deciding he's licked. As he disengages, he can get violently prodded on his way by the victory-flushed winner. That's why Jim's buck was so battered in the behind. A full-grown northern whitetail is a formidably strong creature. Large men attacked by "tame" but rut-crazed bucks have been killed, badly hurt, or have escaped only after Homeric struggles. John Madson, in his excellent monograph on whitetails published by Olin (Winchester-Western), tells of one penned whitetail buck who killed an unready doe, badly wounded another doe, killed two other bucks (one of them big), and then attacked and almost killed his 200-pound farmer-owner in the pen. The farmer escaped only when two other men rushed to his aid and beat off the combat-crazed buck with a pick handle and a 2X4 club. In another case, a rut-mad buck in a pen with three does not ready to breed killed them all one night with antler attacks.

I've never seen a buck duel in the wild. Few people have. However, after deer season, I once found the scene of such a battle. In a circle about 30 or 40 feet in diameter, the ground was as thoroughly churned as if rototilled. It was in a swamp of tag alders, tough, elastic shrubbery. Even so, every alder bush in that circle was smashed to pieces. The battle probably lasted for hours. Deer hair was all over the arena. But a careful search around the gladiatorial area revealed no dead buck.

HOW TO "RATTLE UP" A BUCK

For hunters, the frequency of whitetail buck fights gives rise to the fascinating use of handheld antlers to "rattle up" deer by simu-

Antler rattling, a specialty of some Texas hunters, hasn't caught on very much among northern deer hunters, but it may be well worth trying when seasons coincide with rutting periods.

lating a fight. It's a standard hunting practice, especially among Texas hunters, and is highly effective. It hasn't worked for me, probably because I've only tried it a couple of times.

Texas rancher and outdoor writer Byron Dalrymple, in his excellent book *Deer Hunting with Dalrymple,* goes into detail on antler-clashing to attract bucks. He likes to pick an area with both cover for himself and appropriate visibility to spot incoming bucks. After a loud, attention-getting whack with the handheld pair of antlers, Dalrymple crashes them together and rattles tines. Some ground thumping to imitate buck stamping and a raking of a nearby tree trunk are added attractions. After this, sound is stopped, then resumed.

Dalrymple says it works best in early morning and late afternoon, but may bring in bucks anytime on a cool, overcast day. But bring 'em in it does—Byron, with a TV moviemaker in tow, once rattled up 52 bucks in 10 days to shoot film footage since seen by millions of TV viewers. My Kansas friend, Dr. George Halazon, another professional maker of wildlife films, also uses antler-rattling successfully.

What's the secret? We can only guess that a buck, upon hearing the racket, assumes he has trespassing bucks in his home range. That brings him in to fight. Sometimes a pair of bucks duke it out while there's a breedable doe standing by to reward the victor. A smart buck may sneak up to antler-rattling in hopes of eloping with her while the two gladiators are tied up.

Those who have used antler-rattling successfully warn that not all deer respond the same way. Some bucks come head-long, without caution. Others may sneak in and circle in adjoining cover to get the scent first.

A companion technique, using a deer call, seems very spotty in results. Whitetails are not mute. My Minnesota game warden friend, Frank Baltich, relates sitting in a field at night watching for deer shiners and frequently hearing grazing whitetails blatting. It may be their way of keeping track of one another in the dark. But attracting whitetail bucks with a bleating call rarely seems to work, though commercial call maker Winston Burnham of Texas has had some success. As with antlers, I don't feel I've given calling a fair try. Once, I did call in a coyote who tried to leap down on me from a cutbank above. My own guess—unsubstantiated—is that soft use of a deer call might bring in a whitetail buck, thinking the sound was that of a doe bleating to a fawn. But I'd put more faith in antler-rattling.

Some antler-rattlers have had unpleasant experiences being stalked by other hunters. Certainly, common sense dictates wearing bright safety colors when rattling.

TAKING ADVANTAGE OF SEX-CRAZY BUCKS

Another important factor in hunting the rut goes back to the loco unpredictability of bucks then. They'll travel downwind at times, which is highly unusual deer behavior. They'll cross clearings and roads in broad daylight. I got one nice whitetail who slowly crossed an old logging road ahead of me with his nose down in a doe track. He looked neither right or left in his intent fascination with the doe track. I dared not shoot down the logging road but trotted down to where he crossed. Slowing to a tiptoe walk, I peeked past a big balsam into the woods. There he stood, looking back at me, finally alert. As he bounded away, a rear raking shot knocked him sprawling and paralyzed for a coup de grace in the neck. If that buck had followed normal caution of looking up and down a road before crossing in daylight, he'd probably have seen me on the move—whitetails spot movement farther than we credit them—and ducked back without offering a shot.

A doe not ready for breeding must often flee a sex-crazy buck or get killed for non-cooperation, as we've seen. Any time you see a doe in a hurry, be alert for a buck following her, probably closely. Hunters are fond of saying that bucks are smart enough to let does always travel in front to spring any potential ambush. That would call for some abstract reasoning power well above even these wily creatures, I believe. Whitetails after unhunted generations in refuges still typically travel with the buck behind a doe. He can keep track of her better that way or fend off a rival suitor. Among most ungulates, females are the natural herd leaders in any event.

Don't relax after the passage of a doe with no buck. There may be some old rascal cold-trailing her half an hour behind. In this case, he'll likely come slowly, nosing her trail with great concentration. But if a doe comes by in a hurry or if she stops to look nervously at

As the does approach estrous and breeding capability, the normally cautious whitetail bucks grow less cautious and pay attention to little else except the does.

her backtrail, get set for action. There's likely to be a hot-eyed buck on a dead run behind her.

If a doe and her consort buck approach you, the one you have to worry about spooking is the doe. On one of those typical occasions, I watched narrowly, rifle safety off, as a buck and doe (in front) approached my stand area. As they got into my downwind scent cone, the doe froze in frightened alert, ears snapping to full attention. The old buck behind her just blithely closed the gap to lovingly nose her irresistible fanny as I squeezed off the shot.

The bravado of a buck in rut is unbelievable. Back in the days of Minnesota's either-sex hunting, my normally sharpshooting father had a bad day on the stand and emptied his five-shot rifle unavailingly at several does running by. As he disgustedly fished for more shells in his pocket, here came a whitetail buck at full tilt in the track of the does. Despite the barrage of gunfire ahead a few seconds earlier, that buck was bound and determined not to go another direction and get separated from all that potential sex life.

Often a rutting buck will challenge a human hunter with an eerie, whistling snort. Climbing up a timbered mountain in northeastern Washington's Selkirk Range, my oldest son and a hunting companion were stopped dead by the almost screaming snort of a whitetail unseen in young jack firs ahead. While they strained their eyes to spot him, the buck kept whistling violent challenges. Wind prevented him from getting their scent, and he may have been unsure if they were other deer. My son thought fast, grabbed a stick and started lightly whacking a nearby tree to imitate a buck's combative antler play. That didn't bring the challenging buck out of cover, but he began whistling even more. Meanwhile, Pete's companion slipped off to one side to get a flanking view of the jack fir clump. That spooked the buck, who wheeled and made off unscathed. It was an ad hoc ploy by the hunters that almost worked, and is worth bearing in mind in a similar situation. I've had deer give challenge snorts many times (does can do it, by the way) when I had no companion to try a flanking move. Any hunter who learns to imitate that peculiar and indescribable (in print) whistling snort of a whitetail might well be able to call a challenging buck out into the open for an easy shot.

Finally, remember this. Rutting bucks may do some tactically stupid and unpredictable things. But those lapses are of value to you only if you're ready to take prompt advantage of them. Don't be so surprised that you don't react in time. Although I've known a rut-crazed buck nosing a doe track to not even lift his head when my father shot at him and missed, a whitetail buck is capable of suddenly recovering his wits and high-tailing in a hurry. But if you can time your hunting to the period when bucks in your country are rutting, your success chances are probably doubled, or more.

11

Tricks of Trail-Watching

The best whitetail I ever got was a 10-pointer probably hoofing close to 275 pounds. Another hunter kicked him out on opening day without seeing him, the big buck came my way, and I shot him at about 45 yards from a stand.

All that sounds pretty simple. The gimmick is that this particular hunt started some weeks before, when I trekked about a mile back into my favorite whitetail haunts and reviewed the bidding on the deer trails. In a low, brushy area, I found a spot where two main trails crossed. Nearby was a knoll of high ground with a couple of birches close together. Since I'd packed in some scrap lumber, a hatchet and a few big nails, I was able to quickly knock together a tree stand. (This was family land, so I had no compunction about driving nails into our own trees.)

This is trail-watching. "Standing" often refers to the guy posted to head off deer moved by organized drivers. An editor of *Outdoor Life,* John O. Cartier, author of a good book, *The Modern Deer Hunter,* did a survey of various state game departments on what their hunter success studies showed. Cartier's assembled data revealed that more than half the whitetails taken in the Midwest and East are bagged by trail-watchers.

In my northern Minnesota clan, where deer hunting has been a serious matter for four generations, we stuck for years with drives.

Back in the days of less sophisticated deer and fewer hunters, drives were highly productive, even when my dad and his brother Ralph were the only active hunters. A forester by profession, Ralph was a great woods-loper and deer-drive tactician. Dad was an alert stander and a crack shot. They and their occasional guests took lots of whitetails in the seasons between World War I and the late 1940s.

Then things changed. Many more hunters meant smarter deer. Second-growth forests that followed earlier logging and wildfires got progressively thicker and harder to drive. Deer could sneak around the driver, and make it tough for the stander to either see or shoot them. In the early 1950s, we even had a deerless season or two to drive home the reality that the classic deer drives no longer produced whitetails very well.

I proposed a shift to trail-watching, done on a coordinated basis so that each of us covered a main whitetail runway. Once again, we began to get deer. But we had to learn a lot of things about it to enjoy consistent success.

First, good trail-watching begins with thorough scouting to locate key deer trails. We learned the hard way that the more open, vulnerable trails were rarely used by deer in daylight hours but seem to be reserved for safe nighttime travel. Better-screened trails through the typical brush coverts favored by whitetails were the ones to watch.

THE ADVANTAGE OF TREE STANDS

In our northern Minnesota, tree stands were little known in the early '50s. Many experienced deer hunters laughed when I mentioned going up in the air to get deer on the ground. I reasoned that elevated stands probably help disperse the hunter's scent and give the hunter better visibility. Also, with no natural enemies in the sky, forest whitetails just aren't programmed to look for danger from above. (That's not true of western deer and pronghorn, which as fawns are preyed on by golden eagles.)

Minnesota law forbids stands higher than six feet. Even in flat forest country, that's high enough to be a real advantage. Sometimes, a taller stand gives less visibility if it is so high that tree branches and foliage get in your line of sight. After moving to Washington, which doesn't restrict stand heights, I built a couple of

This simple deer stand, despite its lack of concealment for the hunter, has made possible the taking of several whitetail bucks. Whitetails concentrate on potential menaces at ground level and seem rarely if ever to worry about danger from above.

stands that turned out to be too high for optimum visibility. Check your state game regulations on elevated stands.

Texas brush-country hunters build elaborate stands on artificial scaffolds due to a lack of suitable trees. The timber-country hunter can usually find a tree or two for an elevated stand setup. Unless it's your own timber, don't drive nails into the trees. Nails pose a real danger for anyone cutting that timber with power saws, from the logger to the mill crew.

The best system is to use a combination of natural support from live limbs and nylon cord for lashing. The cord won't split and weaken deer-stand lumber as nails often will, and the strong nylon is rot-proof enough to last for years.

Since even moderate-height stands pose danger from falls, rig stout railings for safety. Set at the right height from the stand platform and seat, a railing can serve as a shooting rest or just as a necessary place to lean your rifle when you want to free both hands for coffee or lunch. A wooden ladder or one made of ropes, with cross slatting supported by knots, serves well to get into anything but a very high stand.

Never carry a loaded gun into an elevated stand, whether climbing a tree or a ladder. As tree stands became more popular in the 1950s, state hunting safety statistics showed an alarming rise in self-inflicted gun mishaps caused by climbing hunters dropping loaded firearms.

WHERE TO SET UP A STAND

Whether you use a tree stand or a simple site on the ground, remember that *good* coverage of one or two (at an intersection) key deer trails is the important factor. But don't get greedy and choose a poorly situated trail-watching site just because it covers two trails. It's better to be well-placed on one trail than to be badly sited along two that can't be seen clearly, that offer shooting obstructions, or that are too far off for running game shots in timber. Failure to observe that rule cost me two shots at two nice bucks in one morning. Trying to cover two good lowland trails, I wound up trail-watching from far enough up a ridge to make running shots too chancy on either trail below.

And don't make the similar mistake of picking a stand site just

115

because it offers a good view of a large hunk of territory where you hope a deer will show up. Your chances are better when you're somewhat poorly situated on good deer runways, as opposed to being superbly emplaced where there's only a random chance of seeing game. In our early years of learning trail-watching techniques, at least half our stand sites were wrongly situated and never did produce anything but scenery. Most of our deer came from about three separate stand sites that didn't offer sweeping vistas of the forest, but did thoroughly interdict some well-used deer runways.

Your trail-watching site, even if elevated, should not be upwind from the runway it covers. Winds vary, of course, but there's bound to be a prevailing wind in your area, probably somewhere in the western quarter. Choose a site off to one side or downwind.

REMAINING SILENT AND STILL

Good siting in heavy forest or brushlands may put you very close to the trail, thanks to limited visibility. This means you have to trail-watch in catlike silence without random throat clearing, fiddling around, or moving unnecessarily. You may not see a soft-footed deer until he's only yards or even feet away, and noise on your part can spook him before he ever comes in view.

Smoking creates a highly detectable scent that deer probably associate with humans. Burning tobacco odor never occurs in nature except when those dangerous two-legged predators invade the forest. For the trail-watcher, another problem with smoking is the inevitable noise of fishing around for smokes, striking matches, or clicking a lighter.

Other commonplace noises that a trail-watcher must religiously guard against include coughing, the metallic rasp of opening or closing zippers, and the noise of unwrapping lunch in waxed paper or aluminum foil.

Answering a call of nature is another problem for the trail-watcher. It involves moving around, seriously scent-polluting the whole area, and perhaps being off-guard just when a big buck comes into sight. I'd like to have a dollar for every hard-luck story I've heard about a hunter hunkered down for his morning constitutional, with his gun out of reach against a tree, when a buck (always

When you have selected a suitable trail-watching site, you need only a great deal of patience, the discipline to be quiet, and the ability to stay warm in weather like this.

the size of a Shetland pony and wearing about 22 points in these stories) flashed by.

First, try to get nature's demands done at camp or some place other than where you're going to be trail-watching. Second, don't drink lots of fluids that will require frequent urination. Third, if the need for a bowel movement is felt, do your best to talk your large intestine out of the project for a few hours. Usually this can be done . . . mind over matter.

If all else fails and you have to make a deposit of one kind or another, be sure to go downwind from your trail-watching area. Try to quietly dig out a shallow hole with your heel or a stick. Do your business there, and then (still trying to be quiet) cover it with loose dirt and wet leaves to help keep the scent from broadcasting. Body wastes are one of the animal kingdom's most common bulletin boards, but it's not to your advantage to advertise human presence when you're trail-watching a given area.

It's easiest to stay silent and motionless when you're comfortable. Some kind of seat is almost essential. Sitting on the ground or standing up for a long time is too uncomfortable, and leads to fidgeting or noise-making changes of position. Good trail-watchers are not above packing a folding stool to where they're going to spend hours on end. Even a reasonably portable cushion, as recommended in Chapter 8, is a great trail-watching aid.

Depending upon trees or brush at your site, a blind may be unnecessary. But a blind does offer you some freedom to sneak lunch or coffee without readily observed movement. Be sure your blind doesn't obstruct your vision or shooting.

The need for stealth and alertness can't be overemphasized, not just at the trail-watching site but when approaching it. If you make a racket on your way in, you may alert nearby deer that otherwise might head your way. If a partner comes to relieve you, converse in whispers. The human voice alarms most wild animals and has an embarrassingly long range in the woods.

Along with alertness, patience is the successful trail-watcher's stock in trade. The longer you cover a good trail, the better your chances. You never know when payday will arrive without warning. One moment the forest about you is as lifeless as it's been for hours; then, suddenly, a twig cracks, hoofs thump, or a deer materializes like a ghost without sound. Be alert at any noise. Although a

118

whitetail can move as silently as rolling fog, a big buck, particularly in the rut, may clump along like a very careless, heavy-footed hunter. My least favorite recollection is when I expected my partner to show up, as planned, to take my place while I worked a drive for him. Someone came shuffling with noisy abandon through the brush. I yawned, leaned my rifle against a tree, and stood up to greet him. The noisy arrival was a substantial buck who stared at me for one galvanized instant about 20 yards away. I dived for my rifle, but the buck, switching ends, was headed all out for the Idaho border. He won. I never got off a shot.

TAKING THE SHOT

Even when a buck walks into your long-awaited ambush, you can still blow it. First, make utterly sure it's a legal deer. If it's a doe, don't scare her. There's too much chance a buck is following. He may be so close that he's almost cold-nosing her. Or he may be some minutes behind. If she spooks and stampedes, the buck may bolt or sneak off the other way.

In dense forest, trail-watching often permits one shot only. It had better be good. The range is usually very close, but if the deer suddenly reacts to your presence, a clean miss is all too easy. My favorite trick is to ease the rifle up to my shoulder when the deer is looking another way. I snap off the safety or cock the hammer just as the sight comes on target. If the buck hears the metallic click then, it's too late to do him any good.

The late Kermit Roosevelt relished the practical advice of an old western guide he knew: "None of yer dam' fancy shots, man! Shoot fer the pot!" Although a head shot is tempting at close range, it's rarely advisable. A deer's head is a small part of his anatomy, and subject to abrupt movement just when you're squeezing off the shot. A direct hit messily ruins a trophy you might want mounted, and a poorly placed head shot can break a jaw, allowing escape of a wounded animal that's sure to starve. The neck shot is a better choice. If there's any doubt in your mind, lay a solid hit through one or both front shoulders; and that buck is yours. Even if he survives that shot, his mobility is drastically reduced, assuring time for a coup de grace with anything other than a muzzleloader.

119

The right choice of trail-watching site and good technique during the long wait can often provide a shot at a buck like this at close range.

DEALING WITH BUCK FEVER

The trail-watcher, along with the stander in a drive, is the deer hunter most likely to catch a bad case of buck fever. My redoubtable Uncle Ralph once placed a fellow forester on a good trail, promised to run a buck by him, and did in fact chase one through within half an hour. The stander was so smitten by the buck's close appearance that he went into a catatonic trance and never shot. When Ralph came hustling down the buck's line of march in the snow, the stander still hadn't recovered full power of speech and could only stutter unintelligibly.

That was an extreme case of buck fever. More typically, it's a hot-flash blast of feverish excitement and a case of the shakes. Have your gun's safety location memorized before this happens. The hunter who's taken the trouble to become a proficient target shot has an advantage at this point. Even when he's in a blue funk, learned habits of good marksmanship will automatically assert themselves to make a well-placed shot. I don't know of any prevention for buck fever. I do know that if the day ever comes when a nice buck coming down the runway doesn't give me buck fever, I'll sell all my rifles and take up golf.

Final but important note: Trail-watching is usually best when other hunters are roaming an area. One state's study of hunter success showed that trail-watchers who stuck it out past the usual dawn prime time tended to get deer when other trail-watchers gave up and started moving around or hiking out. That midmorning wave of disturbance moves deer for the diehards still in place on good deer trails.

You may get cold, wet and paralyzed in the haunches from hours of trail-watching, and you're certain to get bored. But all the discomfort and tedium is worth it when that big, hatrack buck suddenly walks into view.

12

Drives That Take Deer

Using one group of hunters to drive game into the hands of another cooperating group of hunters is one of mankind's oldest tactics. Some pack predators such as lions and coyotes use it. Drives like this can be highly effective in smaller forests or woodlots, particularly if deer lack plenty of underbrush escape cover to sneak away easily. But in a lot of American forests, driving whitetails all too often is similar to trying to shovel flies across a room. The deer have space, as a rule, to maneuver out of the drive's pattern and the cover to do this unseen.

The reaction of many whitetail hunters in such situations is to make more complicated drives to close off the escape routes for deer. The trouble is, the more complex a drive, the more problems it presents for everyone except the deer. Napoleon once said of maneuvers that there's always a reason why converging columns do not converge. He might as well have been talking of overly complicated deer drives.

Of course, plenty of hunter manpower can make a drive more escape-proof. In some whitetail states, notably Pennsylvania and New York, sizable hunting crews, often organized as private clubs with their own hunting land leases, classically operate drives as a standard tactic. But there are limitations. In some states, maximum size of a cooperating hunter group is regulated by law. The major

122

problem with big, multi-hunter drives is tactical coordination. If all members of the crew don't know the country well, the drive can come apart at the seams. . . . drivers can get tangled up and miss some key areas in their sweep, while standers may never have gotten to the right places. A lot of autumn's short daylight can be wasted in simply corralling a big crew together after each drive and planning the next one.

A common obstacle for a large hunting crew is that some members of the group don't know the country involved. Or maybe they're not skilled enough in woodcraft to avoid getting lost on a drive. So, these inexperienced hunters are often put on stands. At the crucial time, it develops that they can't shoot, either. While missing a deer is no crime, leaving a stand site before the drive comes through is an unpardonable sin.

Many American whitetail hunters operate in groups too small to thoroughly comb dense areas of forest or to bottle up all escape routes. Small-party deer drives must cope with smarter deer these days too. From firsthand accounts of many elderly sportsmen such as my 77-year-old father (who is still getting his bucks), whitetails in the early days were no four-legged Brain Trust. Back then it was not difficult for a single driver to push deer in a fairly predictable straight line to a partner waiting in ambush.

Increased "people pressure" has changed that. Today's deer are no longer seldom-disturbed, easily stampeded wilderness animals. The number of hunters has drastically increased in recent decades. In my home state, for example, licensed deer hunters jumped threefold from a late 1930s figure of 80,000 (only about two hunters per square mile of deer range!) to a third of a million nimrods in the 60s. The number is still increasing.

More than hunters are intruding into the outdoors these days. Other forms of recreation have exploded numerically—backpackers, cross-country skiers, snowmobilers, trail bikers and other recreational-vehicle users, bird watchers, wildlife photographers, backcountry fishermen, rockhounders and so on.

With more people using the outdoors, deer have developed much better routine methods to safely avoid human contact. No more can you expect to move deer to waiting standers by using the old, straight-line, panic-them-out drives. Successful deer driving today calls for different methods. The key is to understand what routine tricks deer use to circumvent people. A blind rush of panicked flight

Cooperation in a two-man drive produced this big whitetail for a pair of happy hunters.

is a very rare, last-resort system that deer will use to avoid humans. They have lots of other cards to play first.

I do a lot of offseason wildlife photography, in addition to all the deer hunting I legally can pack into a fall. Camera hunting requires getting closer to deer than a gun hunter ordinarily must do. Usually, I camera-hunt with only one or two family members as helpers, so there's no wealth of manpower to push game around for me. Thus, I've been forced to learn a lot about small-party deer drives. In the September 1973 issue of *Outdoor Life*, I first described some of these tactics. They must be good, because in rapid succession the small-party drives I mentioned were picked up by various other outdoor writers.

Seriously, I claim no originality for the drives described, because the same tactics no doubt have been used through the ages by deer hunters in breechclouts, buckskins or L.L. Bean's britches. The important thing is that these drives work. Not always, of course, or even a majority of the time. But often enough to make them worthwhile.

THE CIRCLE DRIVE

The simplest tactic is the circle drive. It works well in dense cover, and it takes advantage of the deer's favorite defense system—circling back to spy on anything he discovers is following him.

Usually a driver and stander in dense forest cannot readily move deer any distance in a straight course from point A to point B. One or two drivers can't stop the deer from doubling back to circle the drivers. I've been on non-hunting deer drives for game-census purposes, where scores of drivers 25 feet apart could not prevent deer in dense cover from sneaking back through the line. On one such drive, I spotted a whitetail actually crawling on its belly through dense brush between another driver and myself.

In the circle drive, the driver simply walks a wide circle through the woods around his partner on stand. If cover is particularly dense, the circle drive should be done two or three times along slightly varying routes. The circle drive is so simple that few hunters will even try it. They'd rather try some grand maneuvers that all too often have as many holes as a fishnet.

The radius of the driver's circle depends on density of cover. In

This stander, waiting for a drive to come through, has chosen a slightly elevated spot atop a downed tree. Tactically useful for short-duration stands during a drive, such a location would, however, be too uncomfortable for several hours of trail-watching.

thick cover, maybe the driver is only 100 to 200 yards from the stander while making the circuit. This results in a fairly short drive. Often, that's the most productive kind. Remember that it's well worth the effort to circle your stander two or three times, since deer hiding in good cover may have to be disturbed more than once before they'll decide to move. In more open cover, the driver's radius may be up to a quarter mile. The circle drive tempts a whitetail to stalk the driver. Depending on how the deer tries to circle the driver, this has a fair chance of revealing the animal to the stander at the hub. Not many hunters are really aware how often they're shadowed by their quarry. Forest deer excel at this. Some of my better photos have been of game that took up trailing me discreetly.

Vital to the success of the circle drive is that the stander get into position *quietly*. His success at this makes or breaks the drive. A common cause of any drive's failure is simply that the deer heard (or scented) the stander getting to his post. When conditions are very brushy, or when dry weather makes for noisy walking, both the stander and driver should meander closely together to the standing area. After leaving the stander there, the driver should retrace the route used in approach and begin his circumferential drive. Unless the deer actually saw this operation, it has no way of knowing that two hunters were involved, one of whom is quietly waiting in ambush.

THE DROP-OUT DRIVE

Another good driving technique that works with as few as two hunters is the shadow or drop-out drive. Oddly enough, this drive works without a stander. Both hunters are moving. The gimmick is tricking any deer ahead to think it only has one hunter to evade.

Here's how it works. Making no particular effort to be quiet, both hunters head upwind together. After a short distance, one hunter temporarily stops. His partner keeps moving about 50 to 75 yards ahead in heavy cover, or farther in thinner timber.

After allowing enough time for the distance to be opened up between them, the dropout or shadow hunter starts following his noisy partner. But the shadow man moves very quietly and slowly, while the man up ahead on point clogs along with plenty of careless clatter.

Deer alerted by the deliberately noisy approach of the front man will circle him to get into a downwind position. Depending heavily on their noses, whitetails almost invariably want to get downwind of a possible menace—such as a noisy hunter—to both identify the hunter and keep track of him.

Concentrating on the noisy hunter, the deer is often cold turkey for the silent partner bringing up the rear. Like most animals (and some people), a deer usually can think about only one thing at a time.

One of my chums was the shadow man behind two noisy partners who were well ahead in the timber. Suddenly he spotted a big buck, moving cat-quiet and looking upwind toward the distant noise of the two front men. My chum simply froze with his thumb on the gun safety. The deer kept coming. When the safety clicked off, the startled buck wheeled to look at the new and totally unexpected problem about 15 feet from him, but that was too late to keep his liver out of the fried onions.

There are some special requirements in the shadow drive. Safety precaution is one of them. That's true in any hunting situation. The shadow man must have a good idea where his partner is, which is one reason that the front hunter makes plenty of twig-cracking, stump-kicking noise. Actually, the deer is almost always spotted safely well off to the side as it circles the noisy advance party. If the shooter isn't sure of the deer's line-of-fire location in relation to the other hunter, he doesn't shoot. That's mandatory common sense in any hunting setup.

The other requirement is that the front man has to go slowly. In fact, he should stop at times . . . but still make some throat-clearing or tree-kicking noise while he's at a standstill. Otherwise, the shadow hunter behind can't keep up without making too much noise himself. The secret, to stress it again, is that the deer shouldn't hear that second hunter bringing up the rear.

ECHELON AND PARALLEL DRIVES

Still another good drive requires two or three hunters moving in staggered echelon through the woods with the wind quartering from the rear. Tail-end Charlie, who is upwind of the others, must be the quietest.

A deer circling around the lead man's approach has a 50-50 chance of crossing ahead of the echeloned rear man. Remember, the deer will almost certainly circle into the wind. This is why the drive should have the wind quartering—that tends to control how closely the deer is going to cut in front of that flanking-but-trailing man.

Often the rear hunter can take a temporary stand off somewhere to the upwind side. That's not as foolish as it sounds, because a motionless hunter is not broadcasting scent over as big an area as a man on the move. If the flanker-turned-stander has a temporary vantage point on a high stump, ridge or windfall, he has a good chance of seeing a deer sneaking around past the other two hunters before the animal stumbles into that stander's scent pattern.

A variation of this is simply a parallel drive. Two drivers travel abreast with the wind coming at a 90-degree angle. Deer jumped by the downwind hunter are often a target for the man abreast upwind, since the deer will probably run upwind, right in front of him. For this to happen, the upwind hunter must be quieter than his partner.

Hunters often try to arrange to drive deer downwind toward standers. That would be ideal, of course, since the deer couldn't smell the standers. And, once in a while, very dumb deer *can* be moved a short distance downwind. But most deer simply refuse that version of what amounts to Russian roulette for them.

Worthwhile drives can be made in a valley or canyon if the wind is coming from a 90-degree or quartering angle. This works best with three or more hunters. Two of them work down the valley from opposite directions, heading toward each other. The third man of the crew takes a stand on the upwind edge of the canyon.

The drivers should move slowly but with no attempt to be quiet. Hearing both of them, and naturally fearing the squeeze play that's obviously developing, a deer will tend to turn upwind and go right up the hillside, exiting the valley. Depending upon the height and lay of the land, the uphill stander's scent may not be readily noticeable to the deer. During most daylight hours, the uphill stander's scent may be borne by thermals right over deer well below, letting them climb uphill almost into his lap. But in late afternoon, descending cooler air would tend to carry the high-ground stander's odor down the hillside, blowing the whole deal.

The drives cited should be modified for local hunting situations.

129

When hunting along a big ridge or hogsback, the shadow drive often works best if the No. 2 or shadow man works along the ridge face, while his partner on point stays on the crest. Which ridge face should the shadow man work, since he obviously can't cover both sides? Again, decide which way a deer (dropping down the ridge to circle the front man) is likely to move, assuming it will head into the wind. Since the ridge course may change direction, or the wind may shift, the shadow man may end up hunting one face of the ridge part of the time and then crossing over to the other face when conditions require it.

In thick, noisy cover, the shadow or staggered echelon drives may not work if it's impossible for the sneak hunter part of the team to move without making a racket. In that case, the circle drive is the best bet, especially if there's a place that offers the stander at least some visibility—a high stump, a knoll or island in a swamp, or even a convenient tree with limbs suitable to sit on for a while.

RULES FOR DRIVES, BIG OR SMALL

Certain basic rules apply to either small party or big gang drives. I base most of these rules on my family's 300 man-seasons of forest whitetail hunting at my tribe's North Woods hunting lodge. Various Nelsons have been prowling the puckerbush there for four generations, ever since my grandfather homesteaded the place. These general rules—based on whitetail behavior, not on a set of purely local conditions—apply in all other whitetail country I've hunted, clean across the continent.

1. Don't try to drive deer very far downwind. The misleading idea is that deer pushed that way won't scent standers. But whitetails depend so much on their noses that they naturally refuse to go very far downwind—any more than you'd walk into a dangerous situation with your eyes closed. No way! Only if a drive is so "tight" that drivers are literally a few feet apart can deer be made to travel downwind. Even then, they'll do their best to break out to the side.

2. Trying to drive deer straight upwind at standers is fruitless, because they're almost sure to scent the man-danger ahead. Instead, rig drives in which the drivers push the deer upwind, while standers are situated off *to the side* of natural deer trails and escape routes. This calls for knowing the country well and carefully siting standers

where they have a clean poke at driven deer while still being situated out of the wind-controlled "scentway" that those deer will be following.

3. Short, well-planned drives are best. Long drives can lead to drivers getting off course, thus leaving wide gaps in the driving line for deer to sneak through. In cold weather, long drives sometimes find standers unable to tough it out motionless until the drive comes through. Also, a physically long drive these days runs too much risk of pushing deer into the laps of other hunters who, accidentally or otherwise, may have infiltrated your drive's area.

4. A lot of well-manned drives make lots of noise. This is not the best way to run a drive, heretical though that seems. If a deer is trying to sneak back through a line of drivers, he's helped enormously if he can tell for sure where each driver is; and a noisy drive certainly reveals this information. Try quiet drives in which the drivers are semi-still hunting, with many silent pauses. That will worry bedded deer into hauling tail much more effectively than a lot of caterwauling that gives your whole "order of battle" to him.

5. With a large crew, far too much time is lost in parliamentary debates about what drive to work next. Appoint the best, most experienced hunter of that area as hunt master to decide what the crew is going to do. If his tactics don't pay off, depose him and try another leader! But don't stand around and hold a political caucus after each drive when you should be out hunting.

6. Don't get hung up on making favorite drives when conditions are wrong for those drives. Example: One of our favorite family hunting drives involves a flat piece of second-growth timber bordered by a big swamp. If the deer choose to bail out and get into the swamp, they're safe. Driving the adjoining timber only works if the swamp is half-frozen, since deer will then avoid it due to noisy ice conditions. All these considerations require knowing your area and its local deer habits, which is a strong argument for thorough preseason scouting.

7. Deer like to play a sneaking, circling game when conditions are quiet in the forest. Then it's easy for keen-eared deer to keep track of drivers' progress. Under these conditions, it's difficult for a small hunting party to move whitetails out of dense cover unless the area is quite small. Here, a circle drive can be effective.

8. One of the few times you can drive deer in a straight line is in windy weather. The wind's noise in the forest ruins the effectiveness

Deer drives are far and away most effective when each hunter knows both the lay of the land and his own specific assignment.

Four cardinal rules for the stander during deer drives: (1) be extremely careful of game identification and shooting direction, (2) get into the standing site quietly, (3) remain quiet on the stand, and (4) don't leave the stand for any reason until the drive is completed.

of deer's hearing, thus making the animals jittery. If frightened, they'll usually take off in a straight line upwind, more dependent on their noses when their hearing is jammed by windy weather. In such conditions, they'll often break cover and run rather than sneak.

9. There is a red-hot seat in hell reserved for hunters (don't call them sportsmen) who chisel in to take stands in someone else's drives. Right next to that hot seat is a perpetually flaming stake. Impaled on this for 1000 years at a time are sinners who impatiently left their assigned stands before their hard-working drivers came through. Repent now, all ye who are guilty.

10. Be sure that all members of a drive know exactly what they're expected to do and for how long or to what destination. Fuzzy drive planning and lack of understanding by those involved lead to wasted effort and even strained friendships at times. Having inexpensively Xeroxed map copies on hand for all hunt members is the best thing since the invention of smokeless powder.

11. Standers must get into position as quietly and invisibly as possible. Whitetails that hear standers in the distance can be counted on to remember them, and will try to avoid going in their direction when drivers start pushing them.

12. Most important of all, stringent safety is required on all drives, large or small. Drivers should wear blaze orange whether the law requires it or not. All hands involved must be safe, responsible gun-handlers and hunters, or the stage is set for tragedy.

* * *

Done properly, the deer drive is a sporting and productive way to take whitetails. But pick your partners thoughtfully, and be sure to rationally match drives to the realities of wind, escape routes and other factors. Finally, don't be afraid to try common sense innovations in your drives, big or small.

13

The Fine Art of Stillhunting

Stillhunting is the term for a slow, quiet (it had better be!) "armed reconnaissance," looking for game. In hunting jargon, it differs from stalking in that stalking usually means to sneak up within range of game already spotted.

Stillhunting is not the most common way to get whitetails, although western mule-deer hunters stillhunt a lot. Nor is stillhunting the easiest way to get a whitetail. But it's the most fascinating and challenging way to hunt forest deer. Any nimrod who hangs up a good whitetail buck by stillhunting is truly a hunter in the fullest sense of the word.

First, understand clearly that stillhunting is not for everyone. Some people never master woodcraft well enough to hack it. In much of the whitetail ranges of North America, either terrain or forest and brush conditions simply make stillhunting impossible. It's no good in dense, wet cover where you can't see 10 feet in front of you, such as a northern alder swamp or a southern canebrake or pocosin. It won't work in dry weather in hardwood forests that have floors covered with noisy, dead leaves. Stillhunting is also relatively futile in an area with lots of hunting pressure, because other hunter movements can blow the whole program for the stillhunter. Stillhunters who must wear glasses can be hampered too much in rain and snow.

Finally, the stillhunter has to move solo. A pair of stillhunters close together make too much noise under any but ideal conditions. That doesn't rule out a pair of forest stillhunters working parallel courses 100 yards or so apart, which can be a deadly combination on whitetails. But paired stillhunting works only if your partner has enough woodcraft to stay on course through the woods and not drift into your sector. Also, paired stillhunters must be coordinated well enough to move at about the same rate of speed. Finally, paired stillhunting means that each hunter has a large "dead zone" of at least 90 to 180 degrees of azimuth that he can't take a shot into without endangering his partner.

WHEN AND WHERE TO STILLHUNT

The best environment for stillhunting is one that offers fair visibility and quiet walking in a natural bedding area for deer. Some evergreen forests are ideal if they're not too brushy. Hardwood forests can be okay once the leaves have fallen and a light snowfall or rain has sogged up those dead leaves for quietness of foot movement. Hill country obviously is better for stillhunting, because the hunter can often scan the opposite sides of ravines or valleys, or he can work along ridgetops and have a good view of terrain below. Stillhunting is also practical in flat country under the right conditions.

One of the best-appearing forests for stillhunting is the mature evergreen woods thick enough to have "crowned in" above, forming a permanent canopy that shades out underbrush. Such park-like forests don't offer cover or food for whitetails, and deer are unlikely to be found there if any alternative is available to them. The stillhunter has to go where the deer are likeliest to be, not just where he'd like to hunt from a convenience standpoint.

Where are the likely deer places? Put yourself in a deer's mind before answering that question, specifically about any area you're familiar with. In warm to hot autumn weather, deer prefer shady spots for daytime bedding. In their fall coats, they're overdressed for the warm Indian summer days that can even prevail into November. In rolling country, there are often "cold pockets," such as shady glens on north slopes, that are highly attractive to deer in warm weather.

In wet weather, deer seek shelter—tall grass, cattail swamp margins dry enough to bed in, clumps of low evergreens or big windfalls. A stillhunter working open timber, particularly ridges, during cold winds, steady rain or snowfall is wasting time. Only by accident is he likely to run into whitetails there.

The worst weather for stillhunting is dead calm, regardless of temperature. At such times I've seen whitetails alerted by human foot-travel noise 200 yards distant; on occasion their effective hearing range may extend farther. Cold, calm weather is bad, for example, because the denser air at lower temperatures easily conducts sound waves. Enough wet snow to make squeaky walking is poor for stillhunting, and crusted or icy snow is ruinous.

CLOTHES FOR STILLHUNTING

After the decision of where and when to stillhunt comes the choice of clothes and footgear. Chapter 2 described in detail why wool is the quietest material for woods travel, and why certain footwear is preferred.

Trousers should be long enough to cover boot uppers down to the instep. Twigs make less noise snapping back against wool trousers than against the boot uppers themselves. Boots should be laced fairly tight. Too tight lacing can cramp blood circulation and cause cold feet, even though the stillhunter as a rule is on the move enough to keep warm.

The top garment should be a wool jacket or shirt. If you're hunting in warm weather, such as that in the South, all this wool emphasis may pose a problem. A flannel shirt of the legal safety color in your state can be substituted. Very soft, old denim britches are quieter than new, stiffer jeans. But I seriously recommend a trial of light wool trousers for maximum quietness. Cast-off wool dress trousers would be fine, particularly if they have a soft-finish weave. Avoid brown or gray for safety reasons.

LEARNING THE FUNDAMENTALS

The basic techniques of stillhunting are simple. Through likely bedding areas, the hunter must work upwind to avoid broadcasting

his presence downwind to sharp-nosed deer. Most of the time, he is wise to stick to main deer trails. Deer hearing his approach on a main trail at first are likely to think he's another deer approaching. Even as spooky an animal as the whitetail isn't a total alarmist. Deer hear plenty of noises in the woods, much of it from other deer. What worries them into vacating an area is an unnatural noise such as the occasional snap of twigs against harder cloth garments. Any metallic noise—such as a hanging pair of binoculars or compass clinking against your gun—will also spook them.

Avoiding unnatural noise becomes an obsession for the stillhunter. He must be paranoid about making even little noises that are out of place in the woods. This includes coughing or sniffling. Smokers are at a disadvantage, because they do cough more than non-smokers. A forthcoming cough can be stifled only so long. When you finally must vent it, try cupping both hands over your mouth and put your whole face close to a tree trunk to help muffle the sound. Blow your nose thoroughly when you first wake up and again before you leave camp or vehicle to enter the woods. This will clean out a lot of mucus that might otherwise cause coughing or sniffling later. Obviously, a stillhunter suffering from a cold is facing a real problem, unless he's hunting in conditions that drown out his nose and throat troubles. Rainfall or wind can "cover" for him to a certain extent.

Rain gear is just about ruled out for the stillhunter, unless the sound of the rain is heavy enough to conceal the tympanic and swishy noises of a rain jacket. Don't use a knee-length rain parka when stillhunting, even though such a garment is fine when on stand in wet weather. Fortunately, a good wool jacket and wool trousers will take a lot of wetting before they let the wearer feel much dampness. An all-day light rain won't go through a medium-weight woolen stag shirt or jacket, particularly if it's been treated with water repellent.

A day pack, very useful though it is, is also a noise problem for the stillhunter. In brushy country, I used to simply carry my sandwiches in a game pocket in the back of my hunting jacket. Nylon or light canvas, from which all commercial packs are made, is just too noisy, unless you're hunting open areas without a lot of brush and tree branches to noisily scrape the pack. In Chapter 8, I cited the

This stillhunter has his rifle ready for the instant action that can erupt without warning, but he'd be better off with the sling removed to avoid catching in brush.

quietness virtues of a custom-made wool day pack. Somewhere in your community, there's probably somebody doing custom sewing who can make one of these for you, using a non-wool pack as a general model.

Wear a sheathed hunting knife centered on the back of your belt. There, it's most unlikely to make any "clink" noises by contacting your gun. Alternatives are to carry the sheathed knife in a day pack, or substitute a good folding-blade knife in your pants pocket.

Don't have a gun sling mounted in stillhunting. The swivel hardware can be a metallic noise source. The sling itself can be a noisy brush-catcher. Finally, if you have a sling in place, sooner or later you'll be tempted—against all common sense—to sling the rifle comfortably over your shoulder. In that position, the upright barrel can catch brush unseen and snap it with a loud, most un-deerlike "thwack!" that will put any buck within 100 yards on instant, quivering point.

Second, chances are you'll jump the best buck of the season when you're carrying a slung rifle. You won't get that slung rifle into action in time to make a decent shot, and what you'll say then will make the recording angels cover their ears. Much better to have a quickly detachable sling that you can remove and either carry in your pocket or strap around your waist under your jacket. When you're dragging out a deer, you can then sling the rifle and have both hands free. Meanwhile, the unmounted sling won't be an impediment or deer-losing disaster for you.

The best way to carry the rifle is in both hands when possible. That's fastest for quick shouldering when a buck erupts. Of course, at times you must shift to a one-handed carry, using the other hand to carefully hold branches away from your head and body for quietness on the move.

MOVING QUIETLY

The challenge of the stillhunt is to move quietly and keep a radar-eyed watch for deer. The trick is to do each one of those things separately. When you take a step, carefully look to see where you're stepping. That's the key to quiet movement. *Then* stop and

140

look long and hard, ahead and to the flanks. By far, the bulk of the stillhunter's time in the woods should be spent standing still, looking and listening for any sign of his quarry.

The mistake many hunters make is trying to go too fast. The stillhunter doesn't cover a lot of ground, except under topographic conditions (hunting big canyons from ridgetops) or weather (wind or hard rain) that allow him to move along without worry about his noise. When walking, take short, deliberate steps. With short steps, you can come down as quietly and slowly as you wish, on the ball of the forward foot, feeling for any twig that could crack noisily. Long steps bring the forward foot down on the heel, likelier to snap twigs or make a soft but audible thudding impact.

I don't use any fixed rhythm of so many steps before stopping to look. Instead, I divide the forestscape ahead into a visibility zone. I carefully study the whole zone, front and sides, sometimes with low-power broadfield binoculars to bring out details under brush or low evergreens. Not until I've thoroughly studied the "prime zone" do I move again.

Don't use a straight course as such, but choose your immediate route ahead for quietest walking. Avoid the litter of dry twigs under half-grown evergreens, for example. If you have to cross an area of dry leaves, see if there isn't a log on the ground that you can walk on. Use discretion on any logs, first quietly testing the bark surface with one foot to see if the bark will slough off— something that can spill you like a banana peel if you commit both feet to such a log. Detour small puddles, hanging windfalls, dense brush patches and other places with potential for making unavoidable noise. Rock outcrops and beds of moss provide the quietest walking available. Going down a logging road, stick to the center crown's grass or shoulders rather than the harder, noisier gravel tracks.

A good stillhunter does all these things and also utilizes cover as much as possible, particularly as he approaches a new "prime zone" he hasn't had a chance to eyeball yet. Your slow progress without "foreign" noises of hard cloth or boot leather scrape and no "clink" of metallic equipment may well convince bedded deer ahead that you are another deer approaching normally upwind. But they're almost sure to be watching. You must see and recognize them before they spot you for what you are.

141

Frequent pausing to silently scan for any sign of game ahead or to the sides is a key to successful stillhunting. By squatting, you can see under many branches.

HOW TO SEE DEER

Looking for deer is an art in itself, and one that successful still-hunters excel at. First, don't expect to see a big animal. Even the larger northern whitetails appear to be the size of big dogs in the woods; they're always smaller than your imagination is anticipating. Second, look for parts of a deer, not the whole critter. A bedded deer is darned hard to spot. It's likely to be holding up its head, however, so watch for any faint flicker of movement in brushy bedding places. The one thing the deer may be moving at the time is its ears. A standing deer may be revealed as an out-of-place horizontal line—its backbone profile—in a melange of vertical lines typical of forest trees and upright shrubs. Look for anything that doesn't "fit" in the forestscape. A black spot in the gray blur of brush may be a deer's nose, for instance.

When you spot what you think is part of a deer, don't start shooting. That's how "mistaken for game" accidents occur, relatively rare though they are. Also, good shooting success depends on making out enough of a deer to pick a good aiming point. I never shoot at a game animal but, rather, at a point on that animal. Even on a running deer, where my crosshairs must be swung ahead, my eye and brain are calculating what *part* of the animal I want to hit. The front shoulder area is always a prime target.

All told, the stillhunter is terribly busy all the time, picking his route for maximum stealth, watching for game signs (such as the appearance of a new buck track), watching with eye-straining alertness for game itself, and listening in the bargain. He also has to be alert to where he's going, maintain his compass course if he's on one, and study the terrain to avoid noisy areas ahead.

SIZING UP WHAT'S AHEAD

In addition, he has to be continually revising miniature "war plans" in his mind, based on where he is and what's ahead. Example: Forty yards in front is a small but thick patch of Christmas-tree-sized evergreens. That's a strongly suspect bedding area. How do I approach it to get a clear shot at a deer that suddenly springs out of there? If I go straight upwind at it, any deer bailing out straight upwind will automatically put the dense evergreen screen

143

Fallen logs still sound enough to walk on can offer both silent movement for the stillhunter and useful extra elevation to see what's ahead. Logs of this size aren't common, but even much smaller ones are a help.

between him and me, preventing a shot or even a good look at him. Solution No. 1: Swing to the right to flank that patch rather than barge straight at it. That way, I'll have a better chance at a buck erupting out the far side. But no, there's a dense, low bed of huckleberry directly in the route of a right-hand swing, and I can't avoid making lots of upright twig-slap noise if I get into the huckleberries. Solution No. 2: I'll swing to the left to flank the evergreen clump ahead . . . yeah, there's a good, solid log that will give me 20 feet of almost silent movement, and there's a low rock I can step up on to give me another two feet of elevation for better visibility, which may be crucial in spotting a deer running or sneaking out of the evergreen clump. . . .

And so it goes, with an infinite number of possible variations on the single theme of stillhunting. You cannot relax when stillhunting. You must stay alert, and you must keep your route and "There's a deer now!" contingencies constantly in your mind.

Some of the best stillhunting is done by simply stopping and taking a stand for a quarter of an hour or so when you come to a place with good visibility or to a main deer trail intersection. Particularly if there are other hunters working the area, there's always a chance that their activities may push a buck past. If you're sitting or standing motionless in the right spot, naturally your chances are better than if you're moving when the buck comes along. Such "stand breaks" also give you the only chance for needed mental relaxation, plus physical rest.

How much ground can a stillhunter cover? To go slowly and quietly, about half a mile per hour is maximum speed in a typical whitetail forest of brush and second-growth timber. Covering ground any faster probably means too much noise. Of course, a stillhunter working ridges and expecting to see deer a couple hundred yards down in a canyon or on an opposite ridge can move faster, since his noise-making is less critical. He can also move faster when wind noise is concealing his own noise. But deer are spooky when it's windy in the woods, so don't overdo your rate of travel at the expense of not using cover and not doing a sufficient job of looking.

The stillhunter simply can't afford many mistakes. It's a game for the experts, although anyone with normal senses can become such an expert. Really quiet woods walking takes practice, but that can be done before deer season when you're doing some profitable pre-season scouting, too. Stillhunting remains the most interesting and constantly exciting way of literally sneaking up on one of the world's smartest game animals and beating him at his own game, played on his home field.

14

Hunting Woodcraft

TRAILING WOUNDED GAME

Not as many wounded deer escape as non-hunters assume. In four decades of hunting whitetails, mulies and Columbia blacktails in several states and Canada, I've taken several dozen deer—exact number unknown. I've lost only two that were actually hit. One was a desperation shot at about 400 yards with a .257 Roberts on a running mulie that one of my partners had already wounded; otherwise, I wouldn't have attempted it. I broke one of the deer's forelegs, but didn't stop it from getting away. The other was a whitetail forkhorn that I have every reason to believe suffered only a minor creasing wound. More later on how I determined that.

Whitetails are moderately tough, but they're not very large animals.

Rule No. 1 in preventing wounded game loss is to use the right bullet. As cited previously, using too heavy a bullet in a given caliber is a mistake, because the lower velocity and likely thicker jacketing of a heavier bullet won't expand as well for maximum tissue destruction and shock.

Rule No. 2: Don't write off a shot as a miss simply because the animal vanished with no sign of being hit. Running game often reacts less visibly to bullet impact than standing game. A standing deer usually winces, staggers, or falls from a solid body hit. If the animal is not alert or alarmed before the shot, it may be knocked down even with a poorly placed bullet, only to get up and run away.

By contrast, deer on the run are usually scared, or they wouldn't be running. In this mental condition, they're full of adrenaline. This strength-producing hormone allows severe physiological shock to take place without immediate collapse or even slowing down. And you may not see the running deer flinch at the hit, because it's already undergoing violent muscular contortions to run or leap.

One old fable is that a whitetail drops its tail when hard hit. That's not true. I've seen mortally hit whitetails keep going without the flag-dropping that's so popular in hunting-camp lore.

If the deer vanishes after you shoot, immediately memorize where (1) the target was at the time you shot, and (2) you last saw it. Pick an outstanding tree, brush clump, horizon feature, windfall or some terrain prominence as a reference point. This is crucially important at longer range and can help in even close-range forest shooting.

Rule No. 3: Now mark your own shooting location. Hang your hat or handkerchief on a bush or whatever before you sally forth to where the shot-at deer was. This way, you can orient things. In some terrain, you can look back at where you think you shot from and be badly fooled without a site marker, misleading you in turn on where to search.

Rule No. 4: Look for hair before you look for blood. A hard-hit deer may not bleed for some distance. But almost always, some hair is blown off by the bullet's entry and particularly its exit (if it does) from the body.

Hair can tell you a lot about where you hit the animal. A case history is the unrecovered whitetail I cited as being only lightly wounded. I shot at that young buck broadside at what turned out to be 280 paces on a snow-covered lake narrows. Badly underestimating the range, I didn't lead him enough as he bounded out onto the snowy ice. At the shot, he humped up, then took off fast for the wooded opposite side of the narrows, while a second shot kicked up snow behind him.

I assumed the animal was gut-shot, from the back-humping reaction. That's bad, but with good tracking snow, there was still plenty of chance to recover him. At the shooting scene, I found lots of hair.

But it was all white hair and long at that. A very small spray of clean red blood was in the snow beyond the deer's track.

At once, my gut-shot diagnosis wavered. Tracking soon confirmed that I was initially wrong about the paunch or abdominal hit. The meager blood sign quit. The deer's tracks through a tangled spruce forest showed that he walked, loped, or bounded freely on all four legs (which he was seen using fully after the shot). He circled to play tag with me in that swamp but never bedded down. Several times, his trail showed that he jumped sizable windfalls and lit four-square and running on the far side. A badly wounded deer won't try leaps like that and often crumples momentarily if it does.

Finally, the trail led to the edge of the spruce forest and then up a fairly steep, open, aspen ridge. My deer, once he broke out of the spruce, had gone up that ridge face like a bat out of hell, bounding all the way. Badly hurt deer as a rule won't climb grades. If they do, it's at a walk, not an all-out run.

I gave up the chase due to failing daylight and retraced back to the lake narrows crossing. Another look at the small amount of blood sign there revealed something highly significant that I should have noticed at the outset. What little blood showed in the deer's trail was all on *top* of snow crystals compressed down in his tracks.

All this made me 100 percent sure that I'd only creased that buck broadside across his hinder under the tail, a Band-Aid category of wound. Blood coming from his body any place ahead would have been trampled down at times by his hind hoofs. A gut shot almost always means darker blood, sometimes heavily stained with stomach or intestinal contents. A whitetail has white hair in several places on his body, but only on his tail and rump does it have white hair as long as that cut off by my bullet. Finally, the hour-long tracking of my "wounded" deer showed every sign of a whitetail operating normally with all systems, including the ability to run full-tilt up a steep, snowy ridge.

So, my conscience is free to this day that I didn't leave a suffering, doomed animal behind. That young buck had no more than a tingling fanny for a few days. In giving him that non-fatal education about the unwisdom of crossing open areas in broad daylight, I did him a favor; and he may have lived to be a whitetailed Methuselah if he stuck with that hard-won lesson!

149

In this case, the hair was one of several clues. Length and color of the hair can provide an educated guess on a bullet hit's location. Basically, whitetails have light hair below, on the inner legs and rump, with darker hair elsewhere. A combination of both the brownish-gray hair and white hair can mean a leg hit. Or it can mean a sharply angled body hit (as from a high tree stand) that cut off darker hair on the upper body and exited to cut white hair lower.

By themselves, these individual clues don't tell the whole story. You have to piece them together, as I had to do with the lake narrows buck.

Keep tracking, even if no blood shows. My firstborn popped his first whitetail at about 25 feet, not yards, with a 12-gauge shotgun slug. Hit squarely in the chest and lungs, the deer went about 50 yards, without breaking stride, before any blood sign showed. At first the sign was just a pea-sized drop of bright red blood, which usually means a lung hit. More drops were followed by a blood trail thick enough to suggest a badly leaking paint pail. Totally bled out, the deer lay another 75 yards beyond. The slug did mortal lung damage, but no blood exited the one hole until the lungs filled up with blood to the slug hole's level. In fact, our initial clue that the excited 14-year-old hadn't scored a clean miss was a great amount of hair where the deer took the hit, even though that was all cut off by the slug's *entry* only.

Examine tracks closely for any signs. An injured leg won't register a normal hoof print. Broken low, it will flop enough to make the track awry from other hoof marks. Also, the location of blood sign on brush or grass can tell you if an animal was hit low (leg) or high in the body.

A classic argument rages about whether to follow a wounded deer at once or to wait, allowing the fleeing animal to bed down and stiffen up with the wound. Most hunters seem to vote for the latter. But there are many exceptions. Late in fading daylight, you'd better not waste any time getting after that wounded deer. Same if it's snowing or raining, or if you're sharing the timber with a lot of other hunters who may intercept your quarry. In such cases, time is not on your side.

If a wounded animal beds down and then gets up to travel again, its subcutaneous fat layer may slide into place to block a bullet hole and cut off the external bleeding, greatly hampering your tracking from then on.

Following wounded game is best done with two hunters—one to track, and the other, clearly enough to one side for fast shooting, watching ahead and to the sides for the wounded quarry suddenly rising up to take off anew. When snow is lacking and blood sign is sparse, mark each drop with a handkerchief, cap or piece of toilet paper before you leave it to cast about for the next blood sign. Otherwise, you can miss the last known sign and thus lose the trail for keeps, particularly if there are other deer tracks about.

When you knock down a deer fair and square, go to it and ascertain that it's indeed very dead. If there's any doubt, hit it again if it's still in sight. You may wreck a bit more meat, but that's better than having an entire "dead" deer suddenly take off for keeps. I almost lost a buck on which I'd shot off an antler without knowing it. The buck went up in the air with such a violent gyration that I assumed I'd made a brain shot, trying for his head as I was. As I got up to him, he suddenly came to, minus one antler, and tried unsuccessfully to escape. (Interestingly, three of us, searching hard for a quarter hour, never did find that shot-off antler.)

When in doubt, search and keep on searching. When my kid brother was a youngster, I had him on a ridge stand overlooking an alder swamp while I drove a running whitetail buck through the swamp. Al fired. He said there was a big flash of white, and the buck vanished.

The swamp was a frightful melange of tall grass, alder brush, water and a million other deer tracks. And we had no snow to help. Five of us looked for a long time. The problem is that even a big deer takes up very little space when it's lying dead. I had faith that Al, a cool rascal with a rifle, had clouted that deer and that the flash of white was the running animal being bowled over sideways or somersaulting tail over teakettle. But the others wanted to quit the search.

The following season, I worked a drive coming through that same big alder swamp to hit the ridge stand Al had shot from. In an alder pocket, I almost stepped on the bleached, scattered bones of a big whitetail. The teeth were in good shape—this was no old deer that died of starvation during the winter. To this day, I'm positive it was Al's "missed" deer and that a little more diligent searching might have turned it up.

That was no wounded game situation. Likely, the deer was killed in mid-air about 60 yards from Al's stand. But it represented the loss of a nice trophy and plenty of excellent venison. So, keep on looking! Wounded deer will sometimes dive right under a windfall, stump washout or into very dense grass as they're about to expire. Folded up dead in such a place, they can be amazingly hard to find. You often have to get within six feet to spot the carcass of even a big northern whitetail; and a small southern deer is even tougher to locate.

Above all else, place your shots well and pass up questionable shots; and you won't have many, if any, wounded-deer situations to cope with.

COMMON SENSE ABOUT SCENTS

Since hunters know that a whitetail's nose is a keen danger detector, lots of thought has been given to masking human odor. It can be done. The most successful hunters I've ever known were two unmarried brothers who ran a little dairy farm. With the addition of red safety vests, they hunted in their barn-chore clothes. In a bachelor establishment, neither they nor the clothes got laundered too often. Both those good ol' boys reeked of cow manure so strong that companions' eyes watered.

But in a crew of good hunters, they had more deer opportunities by far. Whitetails in rural areas smell plenty of cow manure and associate no danger with it. I doubt very much if a deer could detect normal human body odor through the miasma of eau de cow dung that enveloped the two brothers. Although I've pondered that many times, so far I've never wanted a deer badly enough to rub myself down with pasture pancakes to achieve the same effect.

Many scents signal "danger" to a deer's nose. Human scent certainly does, at least in hunting season when whitetails are getting edgier by the hour. I've known hunters who've built bonfires and stood wheezing in the smoke of burning evergreen boughs to saturate their clothes and bodies. Sounds logical, but I cannot attest to its effectiveness. In an area with lots of logging activity, I've always thought that sprinkling a little diesel oil on hunting trousers or standing briefly in the exhaust smoke of a logging truck might mask human odor. Like farm-country deer with cow manure, logging-country deer smell diesel odors much of their lives and have no reason to relate it to danger.

Some commercial scents are sold as "buck lure." I have no idea if they work to sexually attract bucks. Depending on how rank they are, they might conceal human smell. Professional trappers sometimes use skunk musk to stink up an area to hide lingering human odors. Like cow manure, skunk musk certainly would conceal the ripest human body odor. The questions are if you can stand to use it; and do you really like hunting all alone?

One thing I am convinced of is that smokers see fewer deer than non-smokers. Over many years in our hunting crew, I've noted that the non-smokers, young and old, get more shots at deer than tobacco fiends. Deer may well pick up the acrid drift of tobacco smoke more easily than human odor.

If you want to try commercial scents, use some common sense first. A scent advertised to represent apples means nothing to deer in non-apple country. One season I tried rubbing my boots with the sweetish musk from deer metatarsal glands inside the legs. I can't say it doubled the number of deer I saw; and no swollen-necked buck thundered up behind me with rape in mind. Still, some reasonable experimentation along the lines of scent to either mask human odor or attract deer could be promising. Anyone have a used pair of size 12 barn-cleaning boots for sale?

COMPASS AND MAP WORK

My favorite orientation story is about a deer hunter in Georgia who loves to hunt deer and is paranoid about getting lost. He never enters the woods without stringing toilet paper all the way, so he can be sure of retracing his path. So far, he says, his love of deer hunting is undiminished, but he's never been more than two rolls back into the boondocks yet.

Orientation with map and compass is essential to any serious backcountry hunting. You need not hunt big wilderness tracts to get embarrassingly lost. On an overcast day with no sun, I once got so turned around in a 40-acre woodlot that I came out on the opposite side from where I intended to be.

Hunters' compasses fall into two basic groups. One is the simplest type with only the four basic compass points marked on the dial. The other category includes precision compasses with aiming devices to take a reading on distant points and (very useful) adjust-

The fundamentals of using map and compass can be acquired at home as part of pre-hunt training in basic woodcraft.

ments for the compass declination in your area. For short-range woods hunting, the first type is fine. For more serious work, the costlier compasses are better, if you take the trouble to learn to use them.

Before entering any area where you may need a compass, check to make sure that the instrument is working. One season, I had two low-priced compasses go bad. The needle stuck on one, due to a faulty pivot bearing; and the other reversed its polarity so that North became South.

Grade-school geography taught us that there are two "Norths." One is the true North Pole. However, compasses point to Magnetic North, which is just a short distance above Hudson Bay. A compass reading in the eastern or western states will be off several degrees from the true North Pole. Where I live in Washington, this angle of declination means the compass North needle points more than 20 degrees to the *east* of True North. For a New Englander, it would be off to the *west* of True North. For midcontinent use, the angle will be slight or zero.

For short-range work of a mile or two in the woods, you can ignore that declination, unless you need a precision course to hit a small area. With non-adjustable compasses, line up the blue or North-seeking needle with "N" on the compass. Now turn the compass slightly to make that needle veer away from "N" the approximate amount of compass declination for your area. Declination is shown on U.S. Geographic Survey maps, available from large sporting-goods stores or local map retail outlets. For areas east of the Mississippi, order directly from: Distribution Section, U.S. Geological Survey, 1200 South Eads Street, Arlington, VA 22202. West of the Mississippi, order from (same agency) at Federal Center, Building 41, Denver, CO 80225. First order an index of your area to choose maps you want.

The best way to cope with a large amount of declination is to lay out the map on a level surface. Then place the compass on it (don't do this on a vehicle hood or near any metallic mass that can affect the compass). Turn the compass base to align "N" with the north needle. On the Geographic Survey map, there'll be a margin triangle showing True North and Magnetic North. Turn the map slightly under your compass to align the Magnetic North line of the map legend with your compass needle. You now have the map oriented to check topographical features around you to understand the lay of the land. Higher grade compasses such as the better Leupold & Stevens models can be adjusted for angle of declination, which speeds up accurate readings back in the woods.

Next, find your present location on the map. Presumably you know the area well enough to do this, unless you drove into strange country in the dark. Move your compass to that part of the map representing your present location, keeping the needle aligned with the Magnetic North line shown on the map. It may be handy to take a straightedge and draw that Magnetic North line down into the map for alignment convenience. With your compass thus aligned, figure out what the course reading will be from the compass graduations, coarse or fine, to hit an area you want to reach. Remember that to come back, you'll have to follow the compass's reciprocal or 180-degree opposite bearing.

Compass and map orienteering is much simpler than it sounds. You can play around with it at home to get the basic principles outlined above. If it still strikes you as a mystery, stop in at a state or federal forestry office and have a forester explain it to you. They're the master map and compass readers and a very friendly class of civil servants as a rule. Outdoor hiking clubs often hold orienteering classes for anyone interested.

Big hunks of trackless country hold no terrors if you have a compass and confidence in it. Of course, you must know where you're starting from in order to get back. With a little study of the subject, you can learn to run triangular or circular routes in the forest that will still take you out where you started. Carrying a good Geographic Survey map showing land forms and streams will help you keep track of where you are back in the boonies. With such a map and frequent compass readings, I routinely made a four-mile straight-line hunt last fall through dense forest, and came out on a Forest Service road within 100 yards of where I wanted to be. Actually, it wasn't a straight-line hunt, due to necessary detours around swamps and other obstacles, but I took compass bearings to compensate for these doglegs.

Woods navigation by compass includes a time factor if you're making changes of course. When teaching my wife compass work, I made a two-hour circular hunt with her. We came out within 30 yards of our starting point. It's a very simple process. Basically, I divided the jaunt into six 20-minute doglegs, not counting time for resting or having a sandwich, of course. At the end of each 20 min-

A compass is useful only if you know where you started from and which direction you traveled. In strange country, check your start-off bearings before leaving camp or car.

Mastering the basics of compass work is essential for any serious backcountry hunting. Hunter here is using a lensatic compass to take a bearing on a distant landmark to help determine his exact location.

utes, more or less, I'd veer 60 degrees to the left (in this case). Six such shifts times 60 degrees equals 360 degrees, or a full circle. My wife was stunned to find us back where we started, but it dawned on her that the process was both simple and foolproof.

Every hunter using a compass at times is ready to swear that the needle is fooling him. I know one hunter who carries two of them to settle arguments with his own mind about directions. Nothing wrong with that. At least he has a backup compass if he loses one in the woods. But learn to use a compass, which is easy, and learn to believe it, which can be harder. Then you won't be like the Maine guide who swore he'd never been lost, but a couple of times he'd been so badly turned around that he was two miles from his own tracks.

15

All-Weather Hunting Tactics

Two climatic extremes may plague the whitetail hunter. One is hot, dry weather that can even occur unseasonally in the northern states. This can really foul up hunting opportunities, severely limiting both the hunter's options and his chances of getting a whitetail. The other extreme is cold or stormy weather. This may foul up the hunter personally, but it can also make for some of the best deer hunting if the hunter plays his cards correctly.

HUNTING IN HOT, DRY WEATHER

The northern Midwest has one of the chillier climates of the non-Alaskan United States. Even so, about a third of the quarter century I hunted there was too warm and dry for good hunting. Conventional drives are not good in such weather. It's far too easy for deer to keep track of woods drivers and then evade them, given halfway decent skulking cover. It's also too easy for deer to hear standers getting into position.

Trail-watching may seem to be a logical tactic when the woods are so dry and noisy that disgusted hunters call it "walking on cornflakes." The problem is that all the hunters then turn to standing, and no one's moving around to push deer for the stump-sitters and limb-roosters.

160

Stillhunting would seem to be impossible in such noisy conditions. However, such weather usually means that there's a high pressure cell of air in the region, often accompanied by some stiff winds. Then the stillhunter has a sporting chance, since the gusty wind will drown out the otherwise hopeless amount of noise he'll make while moving through dried leaves and grasses. The trade-off is that deer in windy conditions are abnormally spooky. They tend to move beds readily and spend a lot of time alertly watching downwind, knowing that they can't depend on hearing.

When one of those high pressure cells is stationary, there may be little or no wind. One hunting option then is very tight drives in small areas, with the drivers almost within handholding distance to keep deer from sneaking through the line. Single hunters or groups too small for thorough drives can only concentrate on trail-watching at dawn, moving into position before daybreak when the forest floor may be dampened by night dew to make careful movement fairly quiet. Later, take off the rest of the day to go fishing or put up storm windows.

Normally dry, warm Indian summer weather is one thing. Actual drought conditions, such as much of the nation experienced in the mid-1970s, is something else. Dry conditions may not kill off the browse species that deer live on, but it will diminish the nutritional qualities of that browse. Deer often turn to feeding on less-affected foods. A drought year in the forest will frequently find deer feeding at night in irrigated fields and roadside ditches that catch and hold moisture.

In farm and ranch country, extra deer damage to crops can make ranchers and farmers more open-minded about allowing hunters onto their property. Browse in naturally wetter lowland areas in the forest will remain more edible and nutritious than deer foods on higher and dryer ground. All these things can change the localized feeding/bedding habits of the whitetails in a given area. Just the physical drying up of a swamp normally too wet for bedding can mean that other, more-open bedding areas now may be used less.

Drought often finds autumn whitetails feeding near marshy ponds and shallow lakes. Water plants maintain their succulence and food value unless the water they're in dries up completely. Another result of a very dry season is that deer are likelier to browse on north slopes of any hilly country. Plants there will be less desiccated from drought than south- and west-facing shrubs.

Meanwhile, the key factor for the hunter is that drought conditions are likely to change the use of a given range by whitetails. It may even force them to move from their usual locale into a nearby area (lower and wetter land, for example) offering better browse and easier-to-find drinking water.

HUNTING IN COLD OR STORMY WEATHER

Severely wet, cold or snowy weather drives most hunters out of the woods. They're overlooking six reasons that favor this kind of bad-weather hunting:

No. 1 is that snow and chilly weather concentrate deer. During summer and early fall, deer spread out over their home range, eating the best variety of food they'll get all year, from succulent water plants in high summer to early fall mushrooms. When the cold blasts hit, all this changes. Tender leaf browse and berries shrivel overnight. Water plants shrink into bottom-hugging winter forms. Ground stuff like mushrooms and clover may be abruptly buried in snow. Instead of having food almost everywhere, deer are forced to seek new supplies, primarily twiggy shrubs. The important thing for the hunter is that deer are now concentrated where such limited-variety winter foods are found.

In mountain country, East or West, alpine meadows that offered good feeding during the summer heat suddenly become arctic environments. Does and fawns leave hill country first, while bucks linger longer. But even if the first snow and cold weather doesn't kick out the bucks, they'll move when the rutting season begins, as we saw in Chapter 10.

Advantage No. 2 for the hunter is that cold weather also forces deer to spend more time feeding. They need more food when temperatures drop, and their food options, as we've seen, are more limited. They must spend more hours moving around to get nourishment, and can be seen more often in daylight hours. Any whitetail on the move is far more vulnerable to the hunter than a deer bedded down.

This is all the more true when a storm approaches. Deer, like other wildlife, seem to be sensitive to barometric pressure drops preceding bad weather. Up to a full day before a major storm, they'll restlessly move about, feeding heavily into midday at times, stoking

162

Cold-weather deer hunting can sometimes look tougher than it is. For the well-dressed hunter, weather like this offers some real tactical advantages over hunting in warm, dry conditions.

up for the added metabolic demands they'll face in severe weather when they won't want to move about to feed. Conversely, the end of a storm sees deer activity increase to make up for feeding time lost when weather had them holed up in shelter.

This kind of weather is most pronounced in the northern tier of states, and it may be severe enough to make the hunters head home either for comfort or sheer survival. Anyone who saw an early season killer storm like the historic Armistice Day blizzard of 1940 knows what I mean. But the worst of storms end eventually, and that's the time to hit the timber.

You'll have the enormous advantage of knowing almost exactly where the deer are, if you know your hunting area at all. First, deer will be found in the thickest cover during a snowstorm. Second, after the storm, they'll stick fairly close to dense cover between feedings. Why? Because such snowstorms are almost always followed by a high pressure cell's colder weather. I'm convinced that deer take a while to become acclimated to winter. They seem particularly sensitive to that first blast of really chilly weather in autumn, and use the best available cover for a while.

Sometimes such a storm degenerates into freezing rain which can ruin hunting. The snow becomes noisy when wet and may freeze with a crust. In that case, the hunter on the move might just as well drag empty tin cans in terms of making a racket.

Although southern hunters may never hunt in snow, the South has wet cold fronts that force deer into the same kind of ritual. I've camera-hunted in southeast Oklahoma's "Little Dixie," timbered hill country full of whitetails, in cold, wet, November weather and found that this climate holed up deer as much as would a blue norther in Texas or a Canadian storm sweeping into the Northwest or Lakes States.

None of this is the same as the midwinter yarding phenomenon of the North, when deep snow immobilizes whitetails in limited areas. Mountain country excepted, autumn storms usually don't bring that much snow. Deer can still move about. But they will stick to denser timber—young evergreen thickets, if available, be it close-packed spruce, tamarack swamps, hemlock, balsam or pine—trying to avoid wind-driven rain, sleet, snow and plunging temperatures. The main point is that even the non-expert can know where to look for them, and that's a tremendous first leg up the ladder of successful whitetail hunting.

Plus factor No. 3 in cold weather hunting is that it makes rutting bucks easier to find. Cold itself does not bring on the mating oestrus in female deer, as explained in Chapter 10. But when breeding-ready does are bunched by weather on what winter range is available, the bucks will usually be close by.

Advantage No. 4 in cold weather involves freeze-up restrictions on deer travel and escape routes, quite apart from the concentration forced on them by reduced feeding options.

Normally, water is no barrier to whitetails. They like swampy lowlands and readily take to water. A quick dive into a lake or river is the northern deer's only real defense against wolves. The whitetail is a fast swimmer, too. A partner and I once pursued a deer by canoe, in order to get photos, and we really had to bend the spruce to catch up. No waterlogged wolf would stand a chance of catching a swimming deer, even in the extremely unlikely event that the lobo tried it.

When heavy frosts hit, ice formation can be a major obstacle to deer travel. Swamps or semi-swampy forests with standing water will be used by deer only in dire emergencies after the thin, noisy, shin-barking ice has formed. Slow-moving streams freeze well ahead of marshes. However, the combination of spring seepage and current often prevents thick ice from forming at the start. Deer seem to sense the thin ice risk and avoid crossing a newly frozen waterway.

A hunter who knows the area can capitalize on this. Any ice-free crossing—such as unfrozen shallow riffles, a beaver dam or a stream section that's narrow enough to leap across—becomes a natural funnel to deer movement across that waterway. When an overnight mercury plunge meant freeze-up, I planned an early morning hunt where a marshy stream had a beaver dam. My partner dogged out the nearby timber, while I covered the beaver dam area. He flushed out a pair of whitetail bucks that were peacefully bedded down together, despite the rut being in full swing.

The bucks sneaked through the best cover. Then they let the hammer down for a full, bounding run over the beaver dam instead of crossing on ice elsewhere at brushier sections of the stream. How they knew it had frozen overnight, I can't even guess, unless they found ice there during pre-daylight wanderings. It would be nice to postscript that I nailed the bigger buck in front, who was a monster; but he was too quick for me, and I barely managed to shoot in time to spill his smaller companion.

165

Wet swale edges offer better deer hunting during that first freeze-up. Such swales ordinarily are great whitetail hideouts and travel routes. But again, formation of weak, breakable ice will keep deer out, unless there's no choice. If a deer does get into a half-frozen marsh, it will slow down (unless hard pushed or just shot at), either because it's alarmed by all the noise or because its legs suffer when breaking ice. Ordinarily, however, deer will prefer to skulk on trails bordering marshes. This simplifies the hunter's planning.

Even when ice is solid enough to hold up deer, they avoid it until it's covered with enough snow for good footing. A deer on glare ice can't run and is plagued by slips and falls when barely walking.

Advantage No. 5 from cold weather is the frequent availability of tracking snow, which is a major hunting aid. Many hunters today seem to ignore the advantage of new-fallen snow in tracking deer. Sometimes a hunter will pick up a fresh track at a roadside crossing, follow it for 10 minutes, and then give up. I often see this story written in the snow. Presumably, the chase is abandoned when a deer isn't seen ahead right away. That may take hours of patient trailing. But a hunter with determination on a buck track in fresh snow has a strong chance of getting a shot at that deer, sooner or later.

In addition to determination, the snow-track hunter needs some stamina. Our country-reared grandsires often walked more in a day than many of us do in a month. To them, a mile into the woods was no more than a block's walk to the parking lot is for us. Many modern hunters won't go a mile into the woods. If they did, they'd take two days' rations, full survival gear, write a last will and testament, and file a flight plan with the nearest volunteer rescue squad. Running a study on hunter density patterns, game managers in one major whitetail state did some actual tracking to see how far most hunters foot-slogged it off the roads. Fifty percent went no more than three-eighths of a mile, which is a bit more than 600 yards.

Every northern hunter should read a highly worthwhile book on snow-country whitetail hunting, *How to Bag the Biggest Buck of Your Life,* by Larry Benoit. A New Englander who has prowled those chilly states since childhood, Benoit took 39 whitetail bucks in 41 years, averaging 7.3 points (eastern count) and 192.1 pounds. But he does this by traveling 10 to 20 miles on a deer track, and not just a meager 600 yards. Obviously, this brand of hunting requires good physical condition, woodcraft, knowledge of the country, and a lot of what my Minnesota Finnish friends call *sisu,* or guts. Benoit

166

Late-season deer hunting need not be an exercise in misery. Hunter here is lightly dressed and bare-handed as the sun comes out after a November snowfall that offers fine tracking conditions.

writes that, on a good track, he follows at a walk, trot, run or, when close-in, panther-foots it as quietly as possible.

The key to snow-tracking a deer is that the deer soon becomes aware that something is on his trail. What is it? Since he's almost sure to be traveling into the wind to let his nose radar work, the only way he can really find out is to circle a bit and watch his backtrack for the pursuer. The tracker must carefully watch both sides of the trail ahead, particularly where there's some good screening cover for a smart buck. Then it's a contest between your eyesight and reaction time versus his.

Of all forms of taking the wily whitetail, tracking has to be the best in dry-throated exertion, ongoing excitement for the tracker, and matchless thrill when you suddenly spot that black nose, white throat and big antlers framing the most alert pair of eyes you ever saw. For sheer sport, I'd rate one buck taken that way worth 10 taken from a stand or on a drive. I'll be the first to admit that I've only gotten a few whitetails this way. But I'll remember them long after I've forgotten (as I already have) many deer taken in easier modes of hunting.

Finally, advantage No. 6 of cold weather is that there is reduced hunting pressure. As cited earlier, lots of nimrods head home when the mercury heads down. Reduced hunter competition may not improve the actual hunting chances, since plenty of other hunters on the move can be the patient trail-watcher's best card, as we saw in Chapter 11. But the *quality* of hunting improves. Few of us enjoy hunting conditions resembling an outdoor version of a Macy's basement sale rush. For more solitude, hunt when the cold weather comes.

Cold weather hunting, which comes later in the fall as a rule, is not the dregs of the season, either. Minnesota's experience is an example. When the North Star state had nine-day seasons in the north, 70 percent of the deer were taken in the first three days. By the last weekend, there were hardly any hunters in the woods! Later, Minnesota spread out its hunting into a hunter's-choice split season. That spread out the hunting pressure, and it spread out the deer kill, too.

Another example is Washington State, which has a split season in its northeastern whitetail range, starting with a couple of weeks in October. Late in November, beginning with the Thanksgiving weekend, the season reopens for several days. During one recent fall,

Although this south-facing hill slope doesn't require a hunter to wear snowshoes, the webs are often handy for late-season deer hunting on more heavily snowed north slopes.

the best hunting by far came in that second part of the season, even though no game animal learns faster than the whitetail. A Thanksgiving snowfall brought down the big whitetails from higher hills, and a one-day checking-station count showed that 18 percent of the hunters took bucks—and a preponderance of bigger, multi-point bucks in contrast to the forkhorns that make up so much of any opening-weekend harvest. Among experienced deer hunters, it's an axiom that the best hunting often comes later in the season when the big, old rascals leave their impenetrable hideouts because of the rut or because bad weather drives them down from hill country. This can be as true in the mountains of Pennsylvania or New England as it is in the Selkirk range of northeastern Washington or the numerous whitetail hills of the Rocky Mountain West.

True, severe weather can foul up the hunter himself, as I cited at the outset. A driving snowstorm cuts visibility to nil and may pose survival risks for the far-back hunter. Thick fog or low clouds in hills also ruin hunting visibility. So does heavy snow encrustation on the woods and brush. Sooner or later, that snow accumulation starts dropping off. The repeated mini-avalanches of snow cascading off trees make deer jumpy, and they move around more. Still-hunting can pay off then, since the frequent thud of snowpacks falling off tree boughs masks some of the hunter's movement sounds. When there's a lot of snow, snowshoes may be necessary. Webs are never quiet, but noise can be kept down by moving slowly. When snow is deep enough to require snowshoes, deer tend to move slowly and often will not move until it's too late.

Take care of yourself in cold weather. Chapter 18 explains just how insidious is the danger of hypothermia when you're wet, weary and haven't eaten for some hours. Your gear needs attention, too. Over-lubricated rifles can jam in cold. Quick-release lens caps are essential on a scope in snowy weather.

Given today's better outdoor garb, bad weather hunting isn't all that uncomfortable. I've had more problems with overheating than with being chilled when hunting in some very cold climates. With common sense in preparation, you'll find that the wet or wintry woods environment isn't as hostile as it appears. And it can be very productive for the deer hunter with some *sisu*.

16

Field-Dressing to Freezer Wrapping

In a great deer camp, with an ash log crackling in the stove and the second cup of coffee being served, I heard this story. A youngster shot at a buck, which promptly fell. The elated kid put down his rifle and proceeded to tag the buck's leg. This occurred in Minnesota, where a self-locking metal tag (like those used on boxcar doors) was required.

The kid was too excited to check where he hit that buck. The bullet had walloped an antler a glancing blow, which temporarily KO'd the deer. Getting that tag run through the skin of his lower leg woke the buck and, with a wild rush, he got up and quickly vanished in the timber. The youngster grabbed his rifle and tore after him. Another hunter ahead saw the running buck and dropped it dead.

The excited and almost tearful youngster came charging up, saying, "Hey, that's my deer!" The adult hunter naturally pointed out that there was no other wound on the deer. "Yeah, but here's my tag on him," the kid declaimed.

The adult's eyes bugged out at the sight of the locked tag on the animal. Then he said, "Sonny, I can't see where you ever hit that deer. But if you can run fast enough to tag a buck without shooting him, you sure deserve this one," and walked away.

171

The essential first step after a deer is downed is to carefully make sure the animal is dead. Hunter here wisely approaches a fallen buck from the rear. Deer have been known to suddenly recover, leap up, and run over a hunter approaching from the front.

Seriously, the first rule in game care in the field is to make sure your deer is dead. A friend of mine started in with his knife on an apparently moribund buck. The deer, which wasn't dead, kicked violently and somehow drove the hunter's knife right through his hand. That, he told me, sure smarts.

If a fallen deer is still breathing, don't try to finish off the animal by cutting its throat. A sudden recovery and violent rush by a big buck could leave *you* stretched out on the ground instead of the deer. It has been known to happen.

Another shot is the only safe, humane coup de grace. The best way to do this is to fire a shot into the top of the neck just forward of the shoulders. If the deer is a trophy that you may want mounted, shoot into the spine just between the shoulders, angling straight down through the lungs and heart, rather than put a pair of holes in that part of the neck that's visible in a full-head partial-shoulder taxidermy mount.

In any event, don't shoot the animal in the brain. A powerful bullet at close range makes a frightful mess of the whole head.

It's not necessary to cut the throat of a downed deer, assuming you're going to field-dress it at once—which you should. The ancient throat-cutting ritual presumably is to bleed out the carcass. Why bother? Within a couple of minutes, you're going to bleed it out as thoroughly as possible by removing the lungs, heart and major connecting blood vessels. Besides, throat cutting can ruin a head for taxidermy work, and it looks unnecessarily gruesome.

The only exception that comes to mind is if a neophyte hunter, who doesn't know how to field-dress a deer, has one down and must wait some time for a companion to show up to gut the carcass. In that case, a knife cut low in the throat may drain blood that otherwise could start coagulating; but the problem is that the beginner probably doesn't have any good idea where the big neck artery can be found with a knife.

PROPER TECHNIQUES FOR FIELD-DRESSING

There's more than one technique for field-dressing. I prefer the system where the anus is first cut free for later removal with circular slices, like coring an apple. A slender-bladed knife works best for this, as not too much cutting is needed. You can get in the incision

173

with two forefingers, working them around to free the thin tissue connections between the anus and the surrounding hams.

The deer by this time should be belly up on a piece of level ground or rear downward if the ground slopes. It may help to take a boot lace, gun sling or drag rope and tie one hind leg to a brush or sapling to keep the animal on its back. Start making a very shallow incision with the tip of the knife in the groin area, working longitudinally up toward the chest. Be careful not to puncture the stomach or intestines. The best way is to carefully get the incision started, then insert two fingers, print sides up toward you, slightly apart. These are to depress intestines and stomach. With your other hand, insert the knife, cutting edge up, and gently cut forward between those other two fingers that keep moving with the blade to depress the guts out of contact with the knife point.

As the belly is unzipped, the intestines and paunch start popping out. Pull them clear to get working room. Next, trim away the diaphragm, which is a lateral wall of muscle like a bulkhead separating the stomach from the lungs. Now get up into the lungs to both pull and cut them free along with the heart.

Some care is required here, because you'll be working blind, unable to see the knife. Be careful that you don't cut your other hand in the chest cavity. This is the messiest part of the operation in terms of getting your arms blood-stained to the elbows, and it's a good idea to have first stripped to a shirt, with the sleeves rolled up.

You now have a deer carcass with most of the innards lying outside it. Still connected are the lower intestine, which becomes the anus, and the bladder and sex glands. (Some states require leaving the scrotum attached.) Learning some anatomy as you go, locate that bladder between the animal's rear legs. It's inconveniently tucked into the pelvis and tricky to remove. Deer, I'll swear, go through life with full bladders; I've never found one empty. Remove it without spilling the contents all over your best steaks and roasts. Find out where the bladder connects to the urethra and do some careful surgery to get everything freed up for removal all together. This is the part that always worries me, although I've never leaked a bladder onto the meat yet.

An experienced deer-gutter makes short work of all this and winds up snatching out the bladder through the rump hole left by the removal of the anus and lower intestine. For the beginner, I recommend taking it all out in a forward direction. Getting a buck's penis free for removal is quite a job, because it's solidly secured back through the haunches. Does, naturally, are easier to clean at this point. Just remember that the purpose is to get the intestines and bladder removed without dumping their contents.

Once the deer is emptied out, clean out as much puddled blood as possible inside the gut cavity. Try to lift the front quarters to drain the blood rearward and out, or (on non-muddy ground) roll the animal over on its belly to dump out blood. If there's snow handy, I clean the inside with snow and use a bandanna or toilet paper to wash blood off the backstraps, two longitudinal bands of muscle on either side of the spine—makes 'em taste better.

Don't use water to wash out the gut cavity in warm weather. Just wipe out the blood with a cloth, ferns or handfuls of grass. Water can cause meat souring unless the weather is cold. One exception is a gut-shot deer, where thorough rinsing and drying may be needed.

Cut out extraneous fat inside the carcass now. Next, salvage the heart and liver from the offal. These represent some prime eating. I also remove as much of the tongue as possible at this point before rigor mortis locks the jaws shut. Venison tongue, chilled, sliced and lightly salted after boiling, is a superb hors d'oeuvre.

The animal is now ready for removal. Hopefully, you have a plastic bag folded in your pocket for the heart, liver and tongue. Don't cut a further dirt-inviting opening in the carcass up through the chest until you have the animal ready for hanging.

HANGING AND SKINNING

Hunters argue about whether to hang up the deer head down or up. If the carcass has to be hung outside, it's more easily weather-proofed against rain or snow when hung head up. Otherwise, hanging head down makes eventual skinning easier in terms of keeping hair off the meat. The thick hide of the brisket can now be sliced open, and the chest ribs separated with a very sharp, heavy knife or (easier) with a meat saw. A stick put in the ribs will spread the chest open for better cooling and removal of the remaining lengths of esophagus (gullet) and trachea (windpipe) up in the front chest. If the head is not to be mounted, the chest-opening process can be carried right on up into the neck, to get all that plumbing removed for better cooling and to prevent meat souring.

175

Great uproar is heard among hunters about whether to skin right away. The hide can serve as some protection against freezing (which you don't want to occur before the animal is cut and wrapped) or against the elements, including drying out in arid climates. In warm weather, I prefer to get the hide off quickly (easier to skin when the carcass still has body heat) for fastest cooling. But then the bare carcass should be encased in a bobbinet gamebag for fly protection. Some hunters use a hand-rubbed application of black pepper to defeat flies. A clean tarp is useful to protect a hanging carcass against weather and to keep meat-eating birds (magpies are worst) from attacking it. In an old barn or shed, mice or even weasels will start eating some of your venison for you (in the best cuts, of course). The only defense I know is to hang the animal clear of the ground, using wire instead of rope. Prompt skinning also permits thorough cutting off of bloodshot meat around bullet wounds, a must to prevent early spoilage.

Hanging for several days in a temperature in the 30s ages meat for tenderness. The biggest buck I ever shot was not only big but somewhat old and in full, neck-swelled rut. Even as I pulled the trigger, I had him catalogued as a sausage buck. But a week of hanging (hide on to prevent too much drying out) in about 37° F. in a home garage resulted in one of the more tender and better-flavored whitetails of my experience.

Avoid getting venison dirty or wet (except that water cleaning is okay in dry climates, cold weather, or when the moisture can be thoroughly wiped out with paper toweling). Never transport deer on a vehicle hood, where engine heat could touch off spoilage. And don't wrap with plastic. Plastic sheeting can be rigged as a rain shelter over an outside-hanging deer as long as air circulation is still possible.

Although bad-tasting venison is usually the result of improper dressing or meat care afterward, once in a while a deer is inedible through no fault of the hunter. Some deer can get a bitter flavor from certain browse shrubs. A buck after an active rut has lost weight and is sometimes strong-flavored from either all the doe patrol exertions or stepped-up glandular activity. Amigo George Hess, expert hunter and my favorite bon vivant, once nailed a forest buck that was just naturally rank, either from rutting or the wrong browse. The meat was so strong that it defied any flavor-altering

176

Skinning in a way that prevents hair from getting on the exposed meat is easiest when a deer is hung by the hind legs. But if the carcass must be hung outdoors any length of time, head-up hanging is better insurance against the spoilage danger snow and rain can promote.

cooking tricks. George gave it to a neighbor who had a good hunting dog. The payoff was that even the dog wouldn't eat it!

Any game cookbook and lots of non-game cookbooks have venison recipes galore. Space doesn't permit recipe listings here. But as a standard rule, beware of overcooking and drying out this delicately flavored, fairly lean meat. When I'm in too much of a hurry to play gourmet, my standard venison roast procedure is to wrap the meat in foil with a can of mushroom or cream of asparagus soup added. This prevents drying out. Remove all venison fat before cooking, since it has a peculiar flavor, even on cornfed, farm-belt deer.

BUTCHERING

Actual meat cutting is not difficult. You'll need a sharp butcher knife, a meat saw, a clean board, plenty of freezer paper and tape, and a felt-tipped pen or crayon for marking meat packages.

The easiest system is to cut the deer in half crossways, about at the middle, leaving most of the rib cage up front. Using a meat saw, split the backbone of the hind half, most easily done if the deer is hanging by the hind legs. Trim out back loins by carefully cutting them from the hipbones. The loin meat along the split spine can be filleted out or (my preference) laterally cut with saw and knife into chops. Chop thickness is dictated by the ribs' placement. Don't try to make chops too thin. They're best if thick enough to be medium rare inside when fried or broiled.

Finding the ball and socket of the hip, cut along the top of the hindquarter to take off the rump roast. It's the only hind roast worth cutting off on an animal the size of the deer. The classic beef cuts end up too small when applied to deer haunches. You'll need the meat saw to complete removal of the partially excised rump roast.

On the remaining haunch, remove the exterior membrane tissue and then lay it down on its outside. On the inner side of the haunch, cut in to remove the thigh bone. Cut off the lower leg where the haunch narrows—an obvious place. The boned-out upper ham can be used for a good-sized roast or can be partially sliced into round steak. Bone out the rest of the leg for hamburger.

These steps dispose of the hindquarters. Going to your front half, remove the shoulders. These are easily separated with a knife, since

178

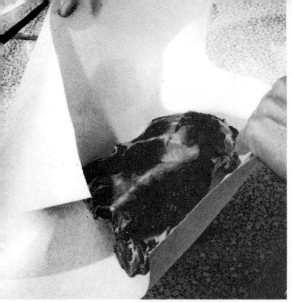

Use plenty of freezer-wrap to seal veni-son cuts against "freezer burn."

Despite the massively swelled neck that tells of rutting activity, author's biggest buck ever turned out to be good eating venison after a week of aging at about 37 degrees F.

they're held on only by tissue. Each shoulder makes a good roast. The legs below are best trimmed for hamburger or stew meat, cutting out any fat, tallow or sinew as you go.

The top of the deer's shoulder fillets out to make good, boneless shoulder loin roast. That leaves only the neck as an untouched piece at this point. Many hunters trim out neck meat for stews or burger. I find that a neck makes an excellent, albeit bony, roast—maybe two from a big deer.

All the rib cage flank meat can be trimmed away for burger. With the fat removed, it also makes superb, oven-dried jerky from any jerky recipe. Use any other red meat scraps for burger. Wrap chops, roasts or any steaks cut off haunches in freezer paper, allowing plenty of tightly rolled paper to overlap and make the packages airtight against freezer burn. Seal them with tape and mark package contents as you go.

The best way to freeze a cut-up deer is in the very cold "sharp room" of a commercial locker plant, then transfer it to your home freezer. The faster the meat freezes, the better. The typical freezer unit on a home refrigerator is not really very cold and may take a long time to freeze a large batch of meat.

Elapsed time on this job is about an hour for two people, one cutting and one wrapping. A professional meat cutter would do it in minutes, of course. But take your time, do good work, wrap the freezer packages tightly, and enjoy all those fantasies about tender chops and juicy, fine-textured roasts. You can almost empathize with medieval nobility who executed deer poachers.

17

How to Train Your Best Hunting Partner

The most enjoyable task a serious deer hunter can face is the job of training someone in his own family—wife or youngster—to be a deer hunter, too. Or more than just a deer hunter . . . a genuine sportsman in the full sense of the word (sexual gender notwithstanding).

Sex makes no real difference in love of the hunting field and not much difference in hunting capability. Girls and women can hack it very well. Granted, they have to be trained right, but that's true of their male counterparts too. Sometimes I've detected an unspoken fear among both husbands and wives that if the little woman takes up hunting, she becomes an unfeminine tomboy. That's ridiculous. My wife is a better rifle shot than many male hunters I've known, has a better spotting eye and listening ear for game than I do, and remains all woman, I kid you not.

TEACHING YOUR YOUNGSTER HOW TO HUNT

Even though most states have a minimum age for a youngster to legally hunt (usually after a state-required training course in gun safety), you can start 'em early with some non-hunting outdoor adventures . . . hikes or overnight camping, for example. When you bring home dead game, a young child is first going to ask questions about death. Be honest. The animal is dead in order to make food for the family table. Use the legitimate analogy of the hamburger or pork chops that mom brings home. The only real difference is that the dead meat she produces weekly from a grocery bag is wrapped in plastic, whereas you're bringing home something still wrapped in its natural hide.

Younger children in my experience (five offspring, plus nieces, nephews, and some younger siblings of mine) are not repelled by this. It's only later, when they're contaminated with some of the anti-hunting propaganda in school or from television, that they may get on an anti-hunting kick. Get your side of the story told to your children a few years earlier, and you shouldn't have any trouble.

Safety and Marksmanship

Firearms safety training should start early. With toddlers around, guns should be not easily accessible, and the ammunition should be completely hidden or kept in a locked box, as cited in Chapter 18. Keep the key in your billfold, not secreted where a nosy kid can find it.

My dad was a shrewd one. At gun-cleaning time, I was allowed to help. Ammo was never displayed. The message was loud and clear that guns were never loaded for any reason inside a house. If my father, whom I presumed somewhere close to God as an authority, wouldn't put shells in a gun inside the house, I didn't even dream of doing it. Helping clean the guns and seeing how the fascinating actions worked was quite a privilege, and I was a willing party to the covenant that this was done only under his supervision.

Later, I used the same approach with children of my own. As the boys reached the age of eight or nine, they in turn were given basic rifle marksmanship training, using a .22 outdoors and an air rifle on an indoor range setup. Both guns were scope-equipped to simplify sight/target alignment. At age 12 came introduction to centerfire big-game rifle practice. A Swedish Mauser 6.5x55 mm. carbine was used, with the military butt-stock cut down to youthful arm dimensions. Handloads were used, both for economy and to use fairly light 140-grain bullets to reduce recoil.

Ear plugs were used to protect hearing. For years, shooters were

Offspring well-trained as sportsmen-hunters can double the pleasure a father gets out of hunting.

careless about this, which is why many middle-aged gun nuts tend to be partially deaf. Even better than ear plugs are headphone-style hearing protectors.

As the boys got a bit bigger, other hunting rifles were used with full-sized gunstocks. These included a lightweight Winchester .30–30 lever gun and my Springfield '03 sporter in the normally hard-kicking .35 Whelen wildcat round. With both the .30–30 and .35 Whelen, recoil and ammo costs were reduced by using cheaper lead bullet handloads. The .30–30 had iron sights. These are tougher for the beginner, but since the boys by this time had mastered breathing control and trigger squeeze on scoped weapons, at least they faced only a single learning situation in being introduced to iron sights to further their shooting educations.

At all times, safety was the key point stressed. What I taught them was augmented by each of them taking our resident state's required youth gun-safety training course.

Americans like to shoot. From Daniel Boone to Audie Murphy, we have a heritage of skill with arms to either put meat on the table or defend our freedom. More than once in our history, Americans who were good at the first consideration were effective in achieving the other objective, too. With this tradition, it's no problem in getting the typical American kid interested in shooting as a sport, if he or she has the opportunity. My sons and I spent many happy hours on the range. Shooting offered another opportunity for some genuine togetherness that helped cement our family ties.

Woodcraft

Shooting safety and marksmanship, essential as they are, still make only part of a beginning hunter's education. Woodcraft can be taught to youngsters in offseason camping and hiking. Orienteering with map and compass can be mastered on a kitchen table and practiced afield any time of the year.

The outdoors can be a somewhat scary place to the beginner, particularly a youngster. There seems to be a lot of room to get lost back in the boondocks. Confidence in outdoorsmanship can be built with compassed hiking. If this is done in an area that you plan to hunt later, it offers a leg up on advance scouting for the coming deer season, if you take time to study the area's hunting potential (Chapter 9).

Along with firearms deportment, woodcraft and hunting skills, the beginner must be taught respect for the basic sportsmen's ethic. This covers everything from a fundamental layman's knowledge of game management (for example, why is it sometimes necessary to control deer populations by harvesting does?) to respect for the law, others sharing the sport with you, and property rights. Certainly, your own hunting ethics have to be up to snuff. It's impossible for a kid to grow up with respect for game laws and sportsmanship if dad has brought home illegally taken game. If you teach your youngster that game laws can be scoffed at, he's going to leap to the conclusion that other laws can be violated for personal convenience. Don't wait until you're sitting in juvenile court with your offspring to think about that cause-and-effect relationship.

All this training sounds like a lot of work for a father. It is. Some fathers don't want to take the time to teach their outdoor skills to their children. In that case, they're missing some wonderful experiences.

WIVES AND HUNTING

Wives are a slightly different matter. While most children will jump at outdoor recreational opportunities, including shooting and hunting, some women just don't dig it. Don't shanghai an unwilling or uninterested girl friend or wife into outdoor recreation. It will wind up being painful for both of you.

For various reasons, my wife and I didn't get our program together in this regard until we were living in middle-aged solitude. That's not too late to start with a willing pupil, however. I began with her in much the same fashion already described—gun safety taught in serious detail, and basic marksmanship training with .22 and air rifle.

As her interest and skill grew, I picked out her own big-game rifle. There's a bit of psychology involved in cementing the beginner's interest in guns and hunting by giving the pupil his or her *own* hunting gun. In Jackie's case, I selected a Savage 99 in .284 Winchester caliber (a combination unfortunately no longer on the market). We do more timber hunting than anything else, and—for reasons cited in Chapter 3—a good lever gun is hard to beat there. The medium-weight 99 has a strong and long-proved action and will take a con-

Peggy McLarney, wife of outdoor writer Ed McLarney, is getting her forkhorn buck out to road by herself.

ventionally mounted scope. The .284 round was chosen not just for deer, but also for the elk and black bear of the Pacific Northwest. The availability of such bigger game in our area ruled out light cartridge choices such as the .250 Savage or the .243 Winchester, both excellent for deer but insufficient for elk.

The buttstock had to be shortened to fit Jackie. Then we were ready for familiarization firing and actual marksmanship practice. Quality hearing protectors were used. Aside from protecting hearing, these help prevent the shooter from flinching at the noise.

GENERAL RULES FOR ALL BEGINNERS

Some general rules apply to beginning hunters of any age. Don't start by taking them on very tough hunts. Try to break them in easily. Although firm control in safety matters is a must, don't be a snarling taskmaster or act like a Marine drill instructor when they make other mistakes. The better your training, the less mistakes they'll make. I taught my wife and children such basic woodcraft as how to walk quietly in the woods during non-hunting outings, as opposed to glaring at them for noisy twig-cracking during a real hunt. With training and practice, children and women actually can be quieter stillhunters than full-sized males.

Make sure they're outfitted with proper togs, from boots to hunting caps. This can run into money, but good outdoor garments last a long time. In the case of children, outgrown clothes can be passed down the line, of course. Wives and teenagers can sometimes wear some of your own extra clothes, which reduces outfitting costs. Just remember that chronically cold or wet beginners can lose interest in hunting in a hurry.

Don't push them too much physically. Even sizable teenagers don't have full muscle strength yet. The feminist movement notwithstanding, women are not the physical equals of men. This is no big problem in deer hunting, since it doesn't require very much physical strength. The hardest work in deer hunting is getting a downed deer out of the woods. Chapter 18 tells how to do that without killing yourself.

Particularly with teenagers, treat them as partners instead of permanent underlings. I learned early that my oldest son had a head for shrewd hunting tactics that, with time and experience, made him well worth listening to. My wife often spots game before I do, and her woods hearing is incomparably sharper than mine.

You need not bear the burden of being the fount of all wisdom in these matters. Good outdoors books help instruct beginners and also have a sneaky way of building up their enthusiasm. When I began teaching my wife to be an outdoorswoman, the first thing I did was have her read Bill Riviere's *Backcountry Camping*, one of the best of many camping books available. Next thing I knew, she was practicing campfire cookery in the backyard and getting very good at it.

Although blessed over the years with many fine hunting companions, understandably the ones I've enjoyed most are those in my own family. Their participation with me has at least doubled my own pleasure quotient in outdoors recreation, including deer hunting. Try it for size in your own family.

18

Safety and Survival

Hunting has become progressively safer in the last generation, thanks to legally required safety classes for young hunters in most states. A young adult hunter who took formal safety training as a youngster is statistically safer than his elders who did not.

The great hunting safety bugaboo among both the general public and deer hunters is the supposed likelihood of a stray bullet hitting someone without warning. However, safety studies show that such mishaps are extremely rare, even when the woods are crowded with hunters.

HUNTING MISHAPS AND HOW TO AVOID THEM

The great majority of hunting-gun mishaps falls into two categories. About half the victims clumsily shoot themselves. Remedy: Know the common sense rules of gun safety and practice them—all the time.

The other category includes people who are accidentally shot by someone else. Most are shot by someone in their own party, usually at very close range. This means that the classic "mistaken for game" accident isn't all that common, but that sloppy gun handling in groups, in camp, and getting in and out of motor vehicles does

189

wound and kill a lot of hunters. Remedy: Pick your hunting partners with great care. It's as simple as that. And don't put up with bad safety manners or dangerous horseplay from them.

Safety research also shows that accident-prone shooters tend to have predictable profiles. They've often had gun accidents before, tend to have traffic-accident records and, not surprisingly, have often had safety problems on their jobs. One such chap cited in a particular study had accidental gun discharges three days in a row. On day three, he wounded one of his companions. If he'd been in my party, one of us would have been long gone well before that third day.

Gun safety always pivots around one key rule: *always be careful where that muzzle is pointed,* whether in the workshop, on the target range or in the woods. People can have lapses. Safeties can fail to function. Guns do go off when not intended. All is well, however, if that muzzle is pointed in some safe direction. The hunting cabin roof may get ventilated, but not someone's intestines.

I don't trust gun safeties. On three occasions, mechanical safety systems have failed me, causing accidental gunshots. In each case, the muzzle was not in line with anything human. Individually and cumulatively, those incidents keep me scared for life; and I'm a real bear about muzzle control—mine and those of my hunting companions.

In addition to the first and biggest commandment about constant muzzle control, there are some other standard rules. Don't transport loaded weapons in motor vehicles. It's one of the most common setups for accidents. Never shoot at game that you can't clearly see and recognize to be game.

If you have children in the home, keep your guns under lock and key, not just hidden. Keep all ammunition locked up elsewhere, so that an ingenious youngster doesn't uncover both dad's fascinating guns and cartridges simultaneously.

Make sure you don't get ammunition mixed up in the wrong gun. It's axiomatic that drinking and shooting don't mix. Also draw the line at hunting with badly hungover buddies, whose judgment and reflexes are still impaired from the night before. When you take inexperienced hunters along (kids, wife or chums), make it your primary concern that they handle guns safely. Watch them carefully when they're loading or unloading, the most common time for neophytes to have accidents.

For hunters, firearms safety must be a way of life, not just a pious ideal.

HYPOTHERMIA—THE SNEAKY KILLER

From the central part of the United States on north, the outdoors environment in fall and early winter can be a killer—sometimes a very sneaky killer. The condition that kills is called hypothermia. Think of it as the opposite of heat stroke. It does not mean freezing to death, however. Most hypothermia deaths occur in the 30° to 50°F. temperature range.

The critical factor isn't air temperature but, rather, the rate at which your body is losing heat. Man is a hothouse flower, designed to live with an almost tropical micro-climate next to his hide. In a cool and damp or cold environment, he needs artificial insulation (warm clothing) to stay alive for any length of time. If your core temperature falls only three degrees from its usual 98.6°F., you begin to lose ability to do tasks such as building a survival fire or shelter. At 91°F., speech and more mental processes are impaired. If the core temperature falls into the 85° to 81°F. range, you become irrational or stuporous. From 80°F. down to 78°F., unconsciousness is likely, most reflexes stop functioning, and the heart begins to miss beats. Below 78°F., parts of the brain that control heartbeat and breathing begin to fail. Heart fibrillation occurs, and death soon follows.

To repeat, this can happen in temperatures that are well above freezing. A teenager hunter died of "exposure" (read: hypothermia) when he became lost in my hunting area one recent fall during a two-day rain and wind storm. The temperature stayed in the upper 40s the whole time, too. Wind chill and heat-losing conductivity of wet garments rob the body of heat faster than metabolism can replace it. Even heavy perspiration can set up hypothermia without rain or wet snow.

That's why cotton outer garments are no good for hunting except in warm weather. Wet cotton conducts heat 240 times faster than dry cotton. Wet wool can still help keep you warm to a limited extent, but wet cotton garments suck the heat right out of you, causing hypothermia. Actual tests show that you might just as well be naked for all the good that wet cotton garments provide. Down-filled garments are favorites with hunters in cold climates, but if down gets wet, it packs together and loses its insulation value.

In addition to the right kind of layered clothing (see Chapter 2), the cool- or cold-climate hunter defends himself against hypothermia by avoiding undue fatigue and keeping well-fueled with food. Of course, we all get tired in a brisk day's hunting. The trick is to not exhaust yourself. Strenuous outdoor activity in cool weather can burn up 5000 to 6000 calories. You have to replace this as it goes, since your body can't convert its fat reserves fast enough to keep up, even if you're a chubby little rascal.

Prepare for a hard day's hunt by eating a well-balanced dinner the night before. That allows several hours for digestion and energy conversion, leaving your metabolic tank well topped for the dawn patrol. It's then best to eat a moderately light and sugary breakfast. Too big a breakfast leaves your digestive processes competing with the lungs for available blood supply when hunting exertion begins. Lunch provides the fuel you'll operate on late in the day, when you're fighting fatigue, so make it a good meal even if you're packing it along or preparing it over a campfire. Frequent sugary food nibbling (fruit, candy) helps keep up the fuel supply.

Working hard, your body builds up lactic acid and other by-products faster than it can get rid of them. Five to seven minutes of rest dumps about 30 percent of the lactic acid accumulation. In the next quarter hour, you'll only get rid of five percent more. The trick is to take a lot of short breaks rather than a few long ones.

If hypothermia symptoms start, the best treatment is to remove any wet clothes that are robbing heat, and then dry the skin surface. Reclothe in warm garments or get into a sleeping bag warmed by another person.

The above remedy requires shelter. If you lack shelter, get two or three fires going and sit between them for fast warming. After a fire has burned awhile, it can be raked aside, providing a warm piece of ground to sit or lie upon. A hot drink is a good way to get heat inside the body, even if it's only hot water. But sugary hot drinks (strongly sweetened cocoa, for instance) will provide both heat and quickly converted fuel energy.

Treatment of someone far gone in hypothermia is medically tricky. An unconscious hypothermia patient should be kept prone with the head tilted back to assure an open breathing passage. Run your finger in the victim's throat to assure that his airway is open. Get the victim to medical treatment as soon as possible.

Survival Kits

The danger of hypothermia leads to survival kits. In most American hunting, you're not likely to stay lost more than a day or two before finding your way out or being found. Since you can't clinically starve to death in that time, you don't need a bunch of stuff like small-game loads, snare wire and fish hooks to presumably live off the country days on end.

A survival kit is good only if it's convenient. One of those textbook survival kits containing everything down to a paperback set of the Harvard Classics, to read while awaiting rescue, ends up being heavy. So you find excuses to leave it behind for the day. Sure as shooting, that's the day you're caught out overnight in bad weather.

Here's a common sense, two-pound (or less) set of survival kit items:

1. A sheet of black garden plastic that absorbs any sun heat during the day. Folded, it's as compact as a bandanna. It's five feet by seven feet, weighs just seven ounces, and can be used as a pup tent against rain or snow, as a fire-heat reflector, or as a windbreak. It can also be worn as a parka or poncho or used as a ground sheet on wet ground or snow. Another version is a plastic trashbag with head and arm holes for an emergency windbreaker/rain garment.

2. A lightweight Space brand blanket of aluminized plastic, which folds to a size no bigger or heavier than a tobacco pouch.

3. A 30-foot length of quarter-inch nylon cord for: (a) lashing up a crude shelter; (b) drying wet garments over fire; (c) rigging crude snowshoes; (d) securing your plastic rain poncho about you in high wind; (e) making an arm sling, tourniquet or torso-binding for a broken rib, or tying a leg or arm splint in place; (f) bundling together and dragging firewood to your emergency bivouac site.

4. Lots of big, wooden "farmer" matches in a waterproof container, either commercially available or made from taped-up plastic shotgun shells. Making a fire in wet, windy weather is not a one-match proposition. Take plenty along. A new (but pre-tested) propane cigarette lighter is excellent, but carry waterproof matches as a back-up.

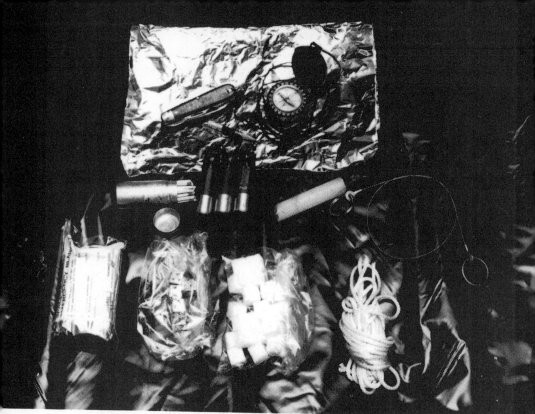

Laid out on a sheet of black plastic (a part of the equipment) is the author's recommended lightweight survival kit: aluminum foil for heating water and for possible signalling use, matches in waterproof containers (a metal photo-film can or taped-up shotshell empties), a lightweight Space brand blanket, bouillon and sugar cubes, 30 feet of nylon rope, a flexible wire saw, and a candle for fire-starting. Knife and compass are shown, but these should be considered only backups for the knife and compass in your everyday hunting kit.

Dead evergreen snags will usually yield pitchy chunks that make excellent fuel for starting a campfire.

5. A braided-wire rope saw (available from Herters or most large sporting-goods shops). This out-cuts a knife on the larger limbs needed for firewood or shelter building.

6. A candle, paraffin chunk or commercial fire-starter strips for getting a lifesaving blaze going when you need it.

7. A pencil and paper to leave a note for any searchers in case you move on from where you are, giving them hour, day and direction you're going, if you know it. (It's often best to stay put if you're truly lost, rather than risk further exposure and energy-sapping fatigue by moving aimlessly. Rescuers in force, from your partners or family on up to the U.S. Air Force, will be looking for you, never fear.)

8. A metal cup or enough aluminum foil to fashion a double-thickness pannikin for heating water to fight off hypothermia or to melt snow for drinking. (Eating snow to allay thirst is a great core-heat robber.) Foil also makes a signal flasher if the sun is shining.

9. As minimum overnight emergency rations, take 20 cubes of sugar and a few bouillon cubes. The sugar cubes weigh only five ounces and pack almost 1000 calories. High-protein nut bars or commercial pemmican adds body fuel of longer duration than that of sugar.

Kit items listed above are for short-term use in chilly but not frigid weather. For prolonged exposure in sub-freezing weather, you'd need more warm gear (lightweight sleeping bag, spare wool socks and so on) and extra lightweight food. For such an expanded, sub-arctic survival kit, select those freeze-dried food items that don't require cooking utensils.

Omitted from my actual survival kit list are a knife and compass, because those should be as much a part of your standard hunting togs as boots and britches. No harm, though, in having a back-up knife and compass in kit. Also left out is a hatchet. It's a risky implement for a person under ideal conditions and very dangerous for a numbed, fatigued user. A small, folding saw is lighter and will produce much more firewood at less effort with almost zero risk.

I, for one, don't believe in digging a snow cave. In most deer-hunting situations, there's rarely that much snow. Instead, look for shelter under a bank or rock overhang, in a hollow log or under a big stump, in a dry culvert (if you hit a logging road or railroad tracks), or under a windfall that can be draped with plastic sheeting, boughs or peeled bark strip (slow process) to shed rain or snow.

Practice fire-building techniques before the season, especially if you live in a chilly climate and hunt country that's big enough to get lost in. Dead evergreen snags will usually yield to your knife enough pitchy chunks to make good starter fuel. Add more dry wood pried out of snags or branches of air-dried, leaning windfalls.

Evergreen woods burn rapidly, so lay in double what you think you'll need for an emergency bivouac. When dry, most hardwoods burn fairly long. Oak is among the best. Ash and maple will burn when green if you have a fire started to ignite them. By contrast, poplar or aspen is almost fireproof when wet.

Emotional state is at least as important as physical condition if you're lost. Don't panic and exhaust yourself. Sit down, take stock, and make rational plans to keep yourself alive and as comfortable as possible in the next few hours. The North American backcountry lacks dangerous animals, except grizzlies in the Northwest—where they're both extremely rare and rarely dangerous. Your main foe is the weather. Use your mental and physical energy to defeat that.

On the opposite emotional scale, don't apathetically give up if you aren't found in a day or so. I know of a case where a hunter lost in Washington State just gave in and curled up to die within short hearing distance of a mainstem logging road that had scores of truck trips shuttling back and forth daily. He was in his resigned-to-die bivouac some days before searchers found him, still alive.

This section on survival is strictly a once-over-lightly introduction. It's a serious, complex subject. If your hunting involves the kind of weather that can kill you if it catches you long enough, study some books on detailed woodcraft and survival and do some off-season practice of things such as fire-building in wet weather. In today's pushbutton energy age, few people know how to start a fire without some actual practice.

THE DEADLY "CAMP CORONARY"

A group of hunters is eating in camp. Suddenly Bill gets a wide-eyed, terrified expression. Frantically clutching his chest or throat, he collapses and dies shortly. Without saying a word, which is significant.

196

"Heart attack" is the immediate guess, and so it may be entered in the vital statistics. But recent studies have shown that many of these dining-table coronaries are really "asphyxiation due to occlusion of the airway by food." In other words, such victims choke to death on a piece of meat lodged in the windpipe.

Rare? By no means. It's the sixth most common accidental death. The Red Cross estimates that almost 4000 people die of food inhalation annually. That's more than the individual toll of lightning, air crashes or all types of firearms accidents. It's many times higher than fatalities from snakebite. Some experts think the real toll is even higher, only disguised in the statistics as "heart attacks." Studies of 51 diners who died abruptly revealed that only one had a real heart attack. The others choked on food.

Hunters in camp are particularly vulnerable. The stage can be set by "camp meat," too fresh for any aging tenderness. Even tenderloin of young deer can be rubbery without aging. Hasty camp cooking adds to the problem. Drinks before eating often figure in food inhalation accidents, because alcohol acts as anesthetic on the gagging reflex. Hence, a dangerously large piece of meat (hungry camp manners ain't dainty) can slide down that would otherwise be gagged up involuntarily. The stage is further set by weariness, probably some laughter, fast conversation with hunting partners, missing molars or poor dentures.

Precautions: Eat only small pieces of tougher foods, such as steak, and chew thoroughly before swallowing. Avoid such foods if you've been making merry with too many glasses of Old Stump-Lifter.

Remedy? First, quickly ask the victim if he can speak. A heart-attack victim can usually talk if conscious, but not so with a food-inhalation victim.

Grasp the victim from behind. Lock both hands just under the sufferer's rib cage, then apply a sudden, hard tug, jerking forcefully against the upper abdomen. This quick pressure forces the diaphragm up, compressing the lungs. This technique, known as the Heimlich Maneuver, may blow the stuck food out of the windpipe. Once blockage is removed, mouth-to-mouth resuscitation can start the victim breathing again. Speed is essential. At most, the victim has about seven minutes to live after choking on food. But even after four or five minutes, lasting brain damage may occur due to oxygen deprivation.

SNAKEBITE AND HUNTERS

Most of us worry too much about snakes. In almost 30 years of hunting the West, good country for prairie rattlers, I've seen only three, even though autumn finds them moving from summer hunting grounds to hill country hibernation. Admittedly, hunters in the Deep South can have more snake run-ins, and with much more formidable serpents than little prairie rattlers.

Even so, snakebite in this country is fatal to only about 3 percent of the victims, although others undergo great suffering and even crippling.

When in snake country in mild weather, keep your eyes open around three key situations: around cabins or outbuildings, when stepping over forest logs, or when clambering around western rimrocks. Never sit on rocks or logs without checking underneath, and never reach up on or step over rocks where you can't see what might be waiting. Deaf to high-frequency noises, I can't hear the thin whir of a prairie rattler's small rattles, so I don't depend on that alarm system. A rattler often doesn't sound off anyway.

If you suddenly look down and see a leg or foot in dangerous proximity to a coiled rattler or cottonmouth, probably the best thing is to move your foot somewhat slowly out of range. The snake is defensively frightened; quick movement might trigger its strike. And there's no ducking the strike of these lightning-fast pit vipers.

Medics don't agree on the best treatment for snakebite. The long-standard system of making X-shaped gashes on the puncture wounds to suck out poison while applying a tourniquet above the bite area has its qualified critics. The remedial gashing may cause unnecessary tissue damage or infection, they say, and long tourniquet application can be dangerous.

Unfortunately, there aren't any practical alternatives in the field. Ice packs applied to a bite area will slow blood circulation and the spread of injected venom, but the hunter afield isn't carrying an ice pack. Thus, the old gash-and-suck system probably is the only choice. Snakebite kits are available with sharp blade, suction cup and tourniquet and give some peace of mind for a few dollars.

If the bitten person has a partner, the victim should stay immobilized while the partner hikes out for help.

Small western rattlers are unlikely to drive their relatively short fangs through ordinary leather boots and at least one pair of wool socks inside. A pair of canvas leggings or gaiters offers some ankle and calf protection. In the Deep South's big snake country, I'd be tempted to wear costlier but effective aluminum leggings. Truly snakeproof boots are available (Gokey of St. Paul, Minnesota, is one source), but are heavy and expensive.

DANGEROUS CAMPSITES

Avoid two kinds of campsites: big, old timber and watercourses subject to flash flooding.

A forest of big, old trees is pleasing to any eye. Usually there's not much underbrush to cut away before pitching a tent. Such forests can be highly dangerous in a windstorm, however. Lethally large branches or whole trees can come down in a storm. A mature evergreen forest showing lots of bare, whitened top branches is an old and dying forest, prone to blowdown. Pick another spot, either in the open or in young trees.

Particularly in the West, flash floods occur with heavy rains. The level ground of a watercourse looks inviting to the camper and, in the fall, the stream itself may be very low or even dry. Don't be fooled. Autumn's equinoctial storms can bring heavy rains that turn shrunken watercourses into swift, dangerous torrents with astounding speed. Also potentially dangerous are banks of rivers whose flow is regulated by reservoirs upstream. Evening power-load demand may require more turbine flow, abruptly raising the river below. If the shore site has little sizable brush or timber and shows dampness of soil, it's probably subject to periodic flooding of this kind and must be ruled out as a campsite.

FOREST FIRES AND HUNTERS

In the last couple of generations, knowledgeable hunters have probably been the most fire-conscious users of forest recreation. Forest fires, according to reliable records, are rarely started by hunter carelessness.

The rules are simple. First, make sure the area you plan to hunt and/or camp in is not closed to use because of fire danger, a common problem in the fall, particularly after frost kills and dries vege-

This well-rigged and well-organized deer camp avoids both the danger of flood-plain location (susceptible to flash floods) and the hazard of old timber (dangerous in a wind storm).

tation. Second, find out if you need any camping or fire permit. If the area you're heading to is national forest, a call to the nearest U.S. Forest Service office will provide information. For non-federal land, check the phone directory for the number of the nearest state forestry office, usually listed under your state's name. Violation of camping or fire-making regulations can ruin your hunting trip with an arrest and fine in some cases.

Next, play it safe with fire. Grind out any discarded smokes. Break wooden matches in two as you discard them after blowing them out. Small campfires are the most useful and safest. Don't ever leave a campfire burning. Douse it with water and spread out the quenched remains to make it difficult for a lingering coal to re-ignite the remaining fuel. If you spot a fire, report it as quickly as possible. Don't refuel gasoline appliances (lanterns, stoves) inside tents or campers or upwind of a campfire. Keep any camp gasoline cached safely away from your fire site, but not in your tent or camping vehicle. If your campfire jumps out of control and starts heading into the woods, fight it first by quickly removing any dry fuel (twigs, dead brush, forest litter) in its path, then go to work beating it out with a shovel, assuming it's still small enough to fight. If not, evacuate and report it.

INDEX